CU00544150

PSYCHOLOGY
THE STUDY OF
BEHAVIOUR

THE
HOME UNIVERSITY LIBRARY
OF MODERN KNOWLEDGE

PSYCHOLOGY
THE STUDY OF BEHAVIOUR

By

WILLIAM McDOUGALL

M.B., F.R.S.

READER IN MENTAL PHILOSOPHY IN
THE UNIVERSITY OF OXFORD

THORNTON BUTTERWORTH, LTD.
15 BEDFORD STREET, LONDON, W.C.2

First Published	April	1912
Revised	July	1914
Second Impression	August	1916
Third "	October	1917
Fourth "	August	1918
Fifth "	March	1919
Sixth "	March	1920
Seventh "	January	1921
Eighth "	November	1921
Ninth "	October	1922
Tenth "	September	1923
Eleventh "	June	1924
Twelfth "	February	1925
Thirteenth "	September	1925
Fourteenth "	August	1926
Fifteenth "	April	1927
Sixteenth "	August	1928
Seventeenth "	April	1929

PREFACE

WHAT is psychology? With what is it concerned? What are the questions it seeks to answer? How is it setting about its task? What are its methods? What progress has it made? Is it a science in an advanced stage of development? Or is it one merely beginning to find its feet, to take definite shape, and to map out clearly its programme of work? Above all, what may we hope from it in the way of addition to our power of understanding human nature and of contributing to the welfare of mankind?

These are the questions which I shall attempt to answer in this book as simply as the difficulties of the subject will permit; hoping that some at least of my readers will be led to feel the fascination of the study and stimulated to pursue it further in one or more of its several branches.

W. McD.

CONTENTS

PSYCHOLOGY

PSYCHOLOGY

CHAPTER I

THE PROVINCE OF PSYCHOLOGY

To define exactly the province of any one of the natural sciences is in no case an easy task. We define them roughly, and sufficiently, perhaps, for most purposes, by pointing to the classes of natural objects which the several sciences study; for example, we say that geology is the science of the crust of the earth. But such a definition is not exact or exhaustive. Geology overlaps with many other sciences: with mineralogy, when it studies mineral formations as part of the earth's crust; with biology, when it studies the fossil remains of animals and plants; with astronomy or cosmogony, when it considers the conditions of the first formation of the earth's crust.

The difficulty of marking out the provinces of the several branches of science is peculiarly great with those which deal with living things. Full and accurate definition would

11

only be possible in the light of complete knowledge. And at present our knowledge of living things is very imperfect. We can see already that, as our knowledge grows, new departments of the science of life have to be created, and that our conceptions of the relations between the several branches must undergo great changes. It seems wiser, then, to determine the provinces of our sciences in a provisional manner only, and with reference to the state of development, the methods of study, and the practical needs, of each one, rather than to attempt any final and rigid definition of them by reference to the classes of objects with which they are severally concerned. Further, we ought to define the province of a science in terms which are as free as possible from theoretical or speculative implications, and which denote only familiarly known objects, generally recognized distinctions, and well-observed facts.

If, in the light of these considerations, we examine the definitions of psychology that have been most widely accepted, we find them to be unsatisfactory. The word psychology was formed from the Greek words for soul and science respectively, and was designed to mark off the study of the soul or of souls as a special department of science. But what are souls? To mark out the province of psychology in this way is to accept a theory of the constitution of human nature which has come down to us from remote antiquity and which is still widely held ; the theory, namely, that each human personality is composed of two very dissimilar parts or principles, soul and body respectively. The soul was regarded as capable of existing apart from the material body and as lending it, during its temporary union with it, all those peculiarities which distinguish the living body from inanimate things. In the earliest times the soul was generally thought of as consisting of a very thin or subtle kind of matter, related to air much as air is related to solid matter. This subtle fluid or spirit was supposed to permeate every part of the body ; and, though it was thus extended throughout the body, it was nevertheless a distinct entity capable of existing apart from it. After the death of the body it continued to exist, and might appear as a dim vapour-like duplicate of it, or ghost. And even during life, this ghost-soul might withdraw for a time, as during sleep or trance, and appear in other places.

Plato, the greatest of the philosophers of ancient Greece, rejected this notion of the soul as a vapour-like duplicate of the body. He regarded the soul as a being of a nature radically different from that of material things;

as incapable of being perceived by the senses, and only to be grasped by the intellect. Nevertheless, he taught that this being exists both before and after its union with the body, which union is but a minor incident of its long career. Aristotle, the greatest of Plato's successors, wrote a celebrated treatise, " On the Soul," which is generally regarded as the first important work devoted to psychology. He rejected the traditional notion of the soul, and regarded it rather as the sum of the vital functions : his attention was directed to the peculiarities which distinguish living beings from inert things ; and to say that a thing possessed a soul was for him but a convenient way of saying that it exhibited some or all of these peculiarities. As to the question whether these functions are attributable to a being or entity that can in any sense continue to exist after the dissolution of the body, he professed himself unable to arrive at any definite opinion.

Through the Middle Ages philosophers continued to debate the nature of the soul and its functions. The most generally accepted view of the soul was one which combined the teachings of Aristotle with Plato's conception of it as an immaterial being that may continue to exercise its functions apart from, and after the death of, the body. And

the natural result of the prevalence of this
view was a tendency to concentrate attention
upon the higher or purely intellectual functions of the soul, and to neglect the consideration of the bodily functions, which Aristotle
had regarded as an important part of the
expressions of soul-life; for these implied
the conjunction of soul and body. In the
seventeenth century, this tendency culminated
in the teaching of Descartes, the founder of
modern philosophy. He boldly asserted that
the bodies of men and animals differ in no wise
from other material things, but are merely
very complicated machines whose workings
are to be explained by the mechanical principles which enable us to understand the processes of other machines. To man alone of
all living things he assigned a soul, and this
soul exercised only the higher mental functions of thought and volition.

The definite formulation of the strictly
mechanical view of nature had led Descartes
to this position; and the rapid progress of
the physical sciences strengthened men's
belief in the all-sufficiency of this mechanical
view, and soon led them to ask—Why, if
animals are merely complex machines, should
man be regarded as anything but one of still
greater complexity? What, they asked, is
the soul? And they answered—It is a

wholly fictitious notion, generated by superstition and maintained by priests in order to strengthen their influence and to support the authority of the Church. In this way Descartes' bold speculations led on to the dogmatic materialism which became very widely accepted in the seventeenth and eighteenth centuries. Philosophers, being thus challenged to provide a scientific foundation for the notion of the soul, found themselves in a great difficulty. Some of them, like John Locke, fell back upon revealed religion as the only sure ground for the belief in the soul. Bishop Berkeley attacked materialism by subtly impugning men's belief in the reality of material things. But one of the most influential writers of that time, the great Scotch sceptic, David Hume, brilliantly argued that the existence of the soul was merely a tradition which had been uncritically accepted, and that no demonstration of its existence ever had been, or could be, made.

Thus, towards the close of the eighteenth century, materialism, and thorough-going scepticism, seemed to be the only alternatives approved by philosophy. At this juncture appeared Immanuel Kant, who offered a new way of escape from this dilemma. He argued that, in perceiving material objects, we can know only their appearances, and that the nature of our conceptions of the physical world is largely determined by the nature of our minds. What we call the world of nature or the physical world is, then, but the appearance to us of some reality of whose real nature we can form no idea, because the nature of these appearances or phenomena is determined so largely by the constitution of our own minds : even the laws of physical nature which we believe we discover, such as the laws of causation and of mechanical operation, are laws which express the nature of our minds rather than of that unknowable reality which appears to us as the material world. He argued further that our minds also are inaccessible to our direct observation, and that we have direct knowledge only of mental phenomena or appearances. Nevertheless, he maintained that, although we cannot establish the existence or describe the nature of the soul by the methods of science, consideration of our moral nature justifies us in believing in its existence as an immortal super-sensible being.

Later thinkers have for the most part accepted Kant's demonstration of the phenomenal character of the physical world ; but they have found his argument in support of the belief in the soul wholly unconvincing ; and subsequent efforts to establish the exist-

ence and define the nature of the soul have
not been generally recognized as successful.

This very imperfect outline of the history
of thought on the soul will serve to show why
it is no longer possible to define psychology
as the science of the soul ; for it shows that
the notion of the soul is a speculative hypothesis, one much too vague and uncertain to
be made the essential notion in the definition of a large province of natural science.
This being the position in regard to the soul,
many modern writers have preferred to define
psychology as the science of the mind. But
this also is unsatisfactory. For, in the first
place, to say nothing of other departments of
philosophy, logic claims to be a science of
mind distinct from, and more or less independent of, psychology; and the definition thus
fails to mark off the province of psychology.
Secondly, the definition is stated in terms of
an extremely ill-defined object. For who can
tell us exactly what mind, or a mind, is ?
When we ask this question, we raise at once
some of the profoundest and most disputed
problems of philosophy.

Some modern writers, recognizing these
objections, propose to improve on this definition by saying that psychology is the science
of consciousness ; for, they say, each one of us
has immediate, direct, and positive knowledge

of consciousness. But to this proposal there are two very serious objections. First, each of us has immediate knowledge of his own consciousness only; the consciousness of other persons is only inferred by him from their behaviour, and imagined after the analogy of his own consciousness. Yet psychology certainly aims at arriving at conclusions which shall hold good of men in general. And when we turn to the animals, this objection appears still more formidable. Secondly, when we study consciousness, we realize that the most complete description of the consciousness of any one person, or even the description, in general terms, of the consciousness of men in general, would not constitute a science, certainly not the science which psychology hopes to become. For such descriptions would not enable us to understand why any particular consciousness takes the form described, nor would it in itself add anything to our power of controlling the course of nature.

Some of those who define psychology as the science of consciousness are content to do so, because they hold a certain theory of the nature of man. They agree with Descartes in regarding the body as merely a complicated machine, and all its processes as mechanically determined; so that every detail of behaviour, whether of man or of animal, is in principle explicable in terms of the bodily mechanism, and falls within the province of physiology, which, in turn, is but a special department of physical science. And the modern exponents of this view do not follow Descartes in regarding thought as a manifestation of a soul informing the machine ; they say rather that consciousness is merely, as it were, a phosphorescent glow generated by the working of certain parts of the machine ; or they say that it is certain processes of the machine of which we become aware in a more immediate and intimate way than the indirect way of sense perception.

Now, if this view were established, the task of psychology might properly be defined as the description of consciousness ; though it would be a work of very small importance and unworthy of the name of a science. But this view of the nature of living beings is a speculation of very doubtful value ; and we have agreed to try to define our science in terms which imply no theories, but rather familiar and unquestionable facts only.

If, then, we ask—What facts are there which are actually observed and studied by the psychologist and which do not fall wholly within the province of any other science ? the answer must be twofold : namely (1) his own consciousness, and (2) the behaviour of men and of animals in general. His aim is to increase our understanding of, and our power of guidance and control over, the behaviour of men and animals ; and he uses what knowledge he can gain of consciousness to aid him in achieving such understanding of behaviour.

We may then define psychology as the positive science of the behaviour of living things. To accept this definition is to return to the standpoint of Aristotle, and to set out from generally recognized facts, unprejudiced by theories. We all recognize broadly that the things which make up our world of perceptible objects fall into two great classes, namely, inert things, whose movements and changes seem to be strictly determined according to mechanical laws; and living things, which behave or exhibit behaviour ; and, when we say that they exhibit behaviour, we mean that they seem to have an intrinsic power of self-determination, and to pursue actively or with effort their own welfare and their own ends or purposes.

The manifestation of purpose or the striving to achieve an end is, then, the mark of behaviour ; and behaviour is the characteristic of living things. This criterion of life is one of which we all make use ; but most of us have not reflected upon it, and we may dwell upon it for a moment with advantage. Take a billiard ball from the pocket and place it upon the table. It remains at rest, and would continue to remain so for an indefinitely long time, if no force were applied to it, no work done upon it. Push it in any direction, and its movement in that direction persists until its momentum is exhausted, or until it is deflected by the resistance of the cushion and follows a new path mechanically determined. This is the type of mechanical movement. Now contrast with this an instance of behaviour. Take a timid animal, such as a guinea-pig, from its hole or nest, and put it upon the grass-plot. Instead of remaining at rest, it runs back to its hole ; push it in any other direction, and, as soon as you withdraw your hand, it turns back towards its hole ; place any obstacle in its way, and it seeks to circumvent or surmount it, restlessly persisting until it achieves its end or until its energy is exhausted.

That is an example of behaviour from the middle region of the scale of complexity ; consideration of it reveals very clearly the great difference between behaviour and mechanical process. As an instance higher in the scale of complexity, consider a dog taken from its home and shut up at some distant place. There, no matter how kindly treated, he remains restless, trying constantly to escape and, perhaps, refusing food and wasting away ; when released, he sets out for home, and runs many miles across country without stopping till he reaches it, following perhaps a direct route if the country is familiar to him, or perhaps only reaching home after much wandering hither and thither.

As an example from the upper end of the scale of behaviour, consider the case of a man who loves his native land, but who, in order to earn his daily bread, has accepted a position in some distant country. There he faithfully performs the tasks he has undertaken ; but always his dominant purpose is to save enough money to enable him to return and to make a home in his native land ; this is the prime motive of all his behaviour, to which all other motives are subordinated. We best understand this last behaviour, if the exile tells us that he constantly pictures to himself his beloved native place and the enjoyments that he hopes to find there.   For we know well what it is to foresee an event and ardently to desire it.   Even if the exile be but a dull-minded peasant, incapable of explicitly anticipating the delights of his return, who seems to be affected merely by a home-sickness which he cannot express or justify in words, we still feel that we can in some measure understand his state and his behaviour. We feel this also of the dog in the foregoing instance, and in a less degree of the animal of our first example. For we, too, have experienced a vague and formless unrest, an impulsion to strive persistently towards an end which we can neither clearly formulate nor rationally justify ; we, too, have experienced how obstruction to such activity does but accentuate our impulse, how successful progress towards the end brings us a vague though profound satisfaction, and how achievement of the end can alone relieve our inward unrest.

These, then, are indisputable instances of behaviour. They are only to be understood or explained after the analogy of our own experiences of effort or striving. No attempt to explain such facts mechanically has at present the least plausibility, or can in any degree aid us in understanding or controlling them. Now the same is true, though perhaps less obviously true, of still simpler forms of behaviour. Let us consider a few in descending order in the scale of complexity.

The migratory bird, arriving in spring, takes up her abode in a coppice, yields to the blandishments of her mate, builds a nest, lays her eggs, and sits upon them, silent and motionless for many days, until the young are hatched. Then, with incessant activity, she

cherishes them, feeding them hour by hour
and minute by minute, until they attain to
independence. With the turn of the year,
her great task accomplished, she faces south-
wards again, and, with tireless wings, returns
across great tracts of land and sea to her
winter home ; there to remain until in the
following spring she comes back, once more
flying thousands of miles to reach the same
hedgerow among all the thousands in our
English counties, and to repeat there the cycle
of her activities. That again is unmistakably
a cycle of behaviour. At every stage the
actions of the bird may be varied in detail
indefinitely ; but always they are dominated
by the same cycle of purposes in which the
great purpose of her life successively manifests
itself—the perpetuation of the life of her race
according to its specific type and kind. If at
any stage her activities are obstructed, her
efforts are redoubled ; destroy her nest, and
she builds another ; take away one or more
of her eggs, and she lays others to replace
them ; attack her young, and she resists you
with all her feeble powers ; shut her up, when
the time comes for her flight to Africa, and
she beats against the bars that confine her,
with ceaseless and varied movements, until
she escapes or is exhausted ; take away her
mate, the indispensable partner of her labours,

and she pines, perhaps even to death. How far the bird foresees the ends of her manifold activities we cannot say; though we have good reason to believe that she foresees at each step no more than the immediate effect or end of each step. Yet we cannot doubt that such trains of activity are more closely allied in nature to our own purposive activities than to any sequences of inorganic nature, and that they are therefore properly regarded as behaviour.

Going a stage lower in the scale of life, consider the salmon which, in due season, having attained a certain stage of development in the open sea, enters the mouth of a river, and ascends the stream to deposit its eggs in the bed of some remote tributary. The ascent of a large and swift river containing many rapids and waterfalls involves ceaseless and varied efforts extending through a period of many weeks, during which the fish takes no food, but consumes the latent energy of the substance of its muscles. This, too, is an undeniable example of behaviour, which we can only understand in any degree in the light of its analogy with our own behaviour, and which is utterly unlike any phenomenon of inorganic nature.

In the great world of invertebrate life, the same great fact of the prevalence of behaviour, or of purposive effort to maintain the life of the species, confronts us on every hand. The solitary wasp hunts assiduously all day long for her prey, and having secured, perhaps, a fat caterpillar considerably heavier than herself, drags it toilfully over, under, or around a thousand obstacles to the nest she has prepared beforehand; there to seal it up together with her egg, that it may serve as food to the offspring which she will never see. The earthworm, coming up from its burrow and finding a leaf upon the ground, explores its boundaries, seizes it by its apex or in whatever manner and position most facilitates its entry to the burrow, and drags it down. And the movements of other worms of even simpler type exhibit the characteristic marks of behaviour; namely, persistent striving with variation of means employed under unchanged external conditions, when the first movements fail to achieve the end. The starfish, turned over so that it lies upon its back, makes incessant and varied efforts with its arms to get a grip upon the ground, and, having done so, rights itself by a combined action of all its parts. And even among the lowliest of all animals, the unicellular and microscopic Protozoa, behaviour is again the rule. The Amœba, a mere speck of formless jelly, on becoming detached from the sub-

merged surface on which it creeps, throws
out long feelers in all directions, until one of
them comes in contact with a solid object;
to this the whole creature then attaches itself,
in order to resume its normal mode of movement. Or, having come in contact with a
smaller specimen of its own kind, it pursues
its prey persistently, making repeated efforts
to englobe it for its own nourishment. The
slipper animalcule darts hither and thither
in search of prey, and may be seen to pursue
other and smaller creatures.

Now let us turn to consider a class of facts
of a somewhat different kind, phenomena
which we cannot so confidently describe as
behaviour. The primary task of every
animal species is to produce eggs, and to set
them in the world under such conditions, and
to afford them such protection, as they need
for their development into perfect repre-
sentatives of the species. This feat, to the
accomplishment of which almost all of the
behaviour of animals is either directly or
indirectly devoted, is but the first part of the
cycle of reproduction on which the perpetuation of the species depends. The consummation of the cycle lies with the egg. The series
of changes through which this consummation
is effected is, in nearly all cases, one of marvellous complexity and marvellous nicety.

Compared with such a series of changes, the most wonderful processes of our machines, such as those by which a garment is woven or a newspaper printed, are relatively coarse and ridiculously simple. But, immensely as they exceed in nicety and complexity the processes of our machines, these processes of development differ in a much more fundamental manner from all purely mechanical processes ; namely, just like the activities of the animal seeking for its prey or returning to its nest, the developmental processes persistently tend towards the end natural or proper to the species, overcoming obstacles and adjusting themselves in a number of alternative ways to peculiarities and changes in their environment, and even rectifying themselves or returning to their normal course after being grossly deflected or disturbed.

These phenomena have been minutely studied in recent years ; and, though our knowledge in this field is still in its earliest stages, we know that the embryo or developing germ of many species may, in spite of being severely mutilated, cut in halves, or completely deformed, restore the normal proportions of its parts and the normal course of development, and may thus achieve its specific end and complete the cycle of activities of which a part only was achieved by the efforts of the parents. In these highly significant respects the process of the building up of the body is very closely analogous to typical processes of behaviour; for example, to the building of its nest by a bird, or to the building of their comb by bees. There is the same persistent tendency towards the specific type which triumphs over obstacles, effects adaptation to unusual conditions, and restores the normal course of events after gross mechanical interferences or distortions. In both classes of process, even the most extreme interferences may be rectified by a resolution or undoing of the stages achieved and a re-starting from the initial stage; the birds rebuild their nest, or the bees their comb, from the foundation upwards; the mutilated germ resolves itself into a formless mass, within which the process of gradual organization of specific structures sets in anew, and so re-establishes the normal cycle and achieves the normal end.

These processes of the bodily growth of animals are, then, closely analogous with truly purposive activity or behaviour, and they present features nothing analogous to which can be found in inorganic nature, the realm of purely mechanical causation. It is true that such processes of growth comprise many details which can be described in terms of physics and chemistry. But the same is true of all behaviour; the most clearly conceived and strongly willed ends of human beings are only achieved by the aid of much detailed process of mechanical type. What is characteristic of processes of both classes is the appearance of effective dominance of the mechanical factors by purposive guidance towards a specific end or goal.

If we make our notion of purposive activity or behaviour wide enough to include these phenomena of bodily organization in the animal kingdom, it must include also the similar processes of plant growth. And there are many good reasons for such inclusion. Biologists are agreed in regarding all plants and animals as having been evolved from the same class of primitive organisms which were neither animals nor plants, or perhaps rather were both. Most plants have little or no power of locomotion or of actively moving their parts. Yet, wherever vegetable organisms have such powers, their movements exhibit the characteristic marks of behaviour; as in the cases of the pollen tubes of many species and the locomotions of some free swimming plants. But, for the most part, the mode of life of plants obviates the need of active movement, and their only opportunity for the exhibition of behaviour is in their processes of growth; and in these processes their marvellous powers of self-direction excel even those of the animals. Of some plants an almost microscopic fragment taken from any part will reproduce the whole plant with all its specific peculiarities. And most plants possess this power of regeneration in a very high degree. Cut away the leading shoot of a larch sapling, and the uppermost branch will slowly turn upwards from its horizontal position, until it continues the line of the stem and, by rapid increase of diameter in its lower part, restores the smoothly tapering form of the stem. Cut a short length from a willow-twig and keep it in a moist atmosphere; no matter what part of the twig be taken or in what position it may be kept, leaf buds will grow upwards from its original upper end and rootlets will grow downwards from the original lower or proximal end. In these and numberless similar instances, the botanist can describe in terms of physics and chemistry many of the details of the process by which the specific form and organization is restored, but the process as a whole completely defies his utmost efforts at mechanical explanation; and we cannot but recognize that it is analogous to the purposive activities of men and higher animals, which are the type of behaviour.

Let us now compare our conception of psychology as the science of behaviour with

the more usual definition of it as the science of mind. It was pointed out on an earlier page that " mind " is itself a word whose meaning is extremely vague, one incapable of being clearly defined except in terms of some questionable and speculative hypothesis. No one can point to a mind and say—that is what I mean the word mind shall denote. And if it is proposed to define mind in terms of consciousness, we are in no better case, but rather worse. For each of us the conscious-ness of any other organism than himself is an inference ; and it is one which is more speculative and uncertain the greater the unlikeness of the other organism to himself. Further, there is abundant evidence that the behaviour of each of us expresses activities of a nature essentially similar to our conscious activities, of which we nevertheless remain unconscious. If, then, we cannot be content to define mind in terms of consciousness, the only alternative is to define it in terms of behaviour. And nothing is to be gained by introducing at the outset of our inquiry the vaguely conceived entity, mind, and placing it between the facts we have to study and our reflections upon them. The conception of behaviour, on the other hand, may be defined in a way which involves no speculative inference or hypothesis, namely, in the way

B

we have attempted to define it above, that is, by pointing to facts open to the direct observation of all men, and saying—This and this is what we mean by behaviour. And such pointing to instances is the only satisfactory, and in strictness the only legitimate, way of defining any abstract notion.

What, then, is, or should be, the relation of psychology to physiology ? Physiology is commonly defined as the science of life or of the bodily functions of living things. But what is life, and what are living things ? Unless we are to define life, in a gratuitously speculative manner, as some imperceptible entity that enters into the bodies of living things, we must say that it is the sum of the processes peculiar to living things. Now the processes by the observation of which we recognize things as living are just those processes which we have collectively designated as behaviour, processes which exhibit a persistent self-direction towards specific ends that subserve the perpetuation of the individual organism or of the species. The province of psychology is, then, according to our definition, co-extensive with the province of physiology And this may be raised as an objection to our definition of psychology ; for physiology is generally regarded as an independent science having its own programme

and methods and history. In modern times the task of physiology has usually been conceived in the way proposed by Descartes, namely, as the working out of purely mechanical explanations of all the processes of living organisms. To accept this conception of physiology is to base the science upon a vast assumption, the assumption, namely, that all the processes of living organisms are capable of being mechanically explained. This is a gratuitous assumption which finds no justification in facts. For no single organic function has yet been found explicable in purely mechanical terms ; even such relatively simple processes as the secretion of a tear or the exudation of a drop of sweat continue to elude all attempts at complete explanation in terms of physical and chemical science. And not only is the assumption wholly un-justified by the demonstration of its truth in any single instance, but it leads those who make it to a logically untenable position. For, when the physiologist has constructed his imaginary scheme of the bodily mechanism, he finds that he has left over as an irreducible surd the facts of human consciousness. And he seeks to escape from the difficulty by ignoring these facts ; that is to say, he boldly asserts the facts of consciousness to be in-explicable by his methods ; he regards them as mysterious by-products of the mechanical operations which he believes to constitute the life of the organism, and in which alone he himself is interested ; and he hands them over to the psychologist, to whom he assigns the exclusive task of describing them.

To define the provinces of physiology and of psychology in this way is just as unscientific as to define psychology as the science of the soul. In both cases it is attempted to mark out the provinces by the aid of speculative hypotheses or assumptions which, though they may be true, can only be shown to be so by great advances of the sciences in question. Nevertheless, it remains true that physiology and psychology, as pursued now and perhaps for a long time to come, are not to be identified. We may express the relation which actually obtains between them by saying that physiology investigates the processes of the parts or organs of which any organism is composed, while psychology investigates the activities of the organism as a whole, that is, those in which it operates as a whole or unit.

In this way we leave to the wider knowledge of future generations the decision of fundamental questions to which at present we can return only speculative guesses, instead of making such guesses the foundation stones of our science. For, in defining psychology as the science of behaviour, we neither affirm nor deny the adequacy of mechanical principles to the explanation of the activities of organisms ; we assume no hypothetical entities or forces, neither life, nor mind, nor soul. We start simply from the undeniable fact that the changes exhibited by material objects seem to be of two different types : on the one hand, of the purely mechanical type, of which the motions of the heavenly bodies provide the grandest and clearest examples ; on the other hand, of the type of purposive action or behaviour, with which each of us becomes familiar by reflection upon his own efforts, his impulses, his desires, and his volitions. It may be that, in the distant future, science will succeed in establishing the truth of the assumption so widely accepted at the present time by an act of faith, the assumption, namely, that all seemingly purposive action is mechanically explicable. If that time comes, psychology will be absorbed in physiology, and physiology in physics. On the other hand, it may be that we shall discover in the inorganic world indications of behaviour which hitherto have remained hidden from us. Or thirdly, it may be that, as a great thinker has lately said, our conceptions both of mechanical process and of purposive activity are false abstractions inadequate to the description of real happenings, and that both must be supplanted by some truer conception. Or lastly, it may prove possible to show that the realm of mind is not co-extensive with the realm of life, and that, within the sphere of behaviour or seemingly purposive activities, we must distinguish a higher type which implies conscious intelligence essentially similar to our own, but of many levels of effectiveness, and a lower type which, though incapable of mechanical explanation and analogous to purposive activity, yet involves no conscious direction, and is therefore not truly purposive.

But, whatever the decision the future may bring, it seems clear that at the present time we cannot transcend the distinction between the two modes of change, and that science is best served by frankly recognizing the distinction where it forces itself upon us, and by carefully establishing it where it remains obscure and doubtful. Physiology, then, may profitably continue to approach living beings from below, that is, from the side and with the methods of physical and chemical science, and to extend to the utmost the reach of mechanical explanations of the processes of their bodies. But psychology must continue to deepen our understanding of the behaviour of all living things by approaching them from above—by applying to them the understanding of behaviour that we gain from the study of ourselves.

The definition of psychology as the positive science of behaviour seems, then, preferable to any other, because it leaves unprejudiced and open for decision in the future the issue of certain fundamental problems which at present we cannot solve, and because it makes use of no ill-defined and problematical notions, such as mind, or soul, or consciousness, but only of familiar facts of observation. And it carries with it also two important advantages. First, it lays stress on the truth that the facts of observation with which we have to deal in psychology are always processes or activities rather than fixed enduring things. Secondly, it prepares us to attempt to understand these activities in a way very different from that in which we aim at understanding physical or mechanical processes ; it makes clear from the outset that we must explain and understand in terms of the end or purpose of the activity, rather than in terms only of the antecedent events. The adoption of this attitude is one of the chief difficulties of the student of psychology, especially if he has been trained in the physical sciences. For

our intellect and our language, the chief
instrument of our intellect, are adapted
primarily and chiefly for enabling us to
appreciate and control the movements of solid
objects in space, or, in other words, for dealing
with the mechanical processes of the physical
world ; most of us, therefore, feel intellectually
at home in dealing with purely mechanical
processes, and we are more fully satisfied with
explanations stated in terms of mechanism
than with those given in terms of end and
purpose ; yet in both cases our explanation
of any concrete event can never be more than
the exhibition of it as a particular instance of
a class of events already familiar to us.

CHAPTER II

THE STUDY OF CONSCIOUSNESS

WE see a child sitting idly on a lawn.
Suddenly he springs to his feet and dashes
into the house, leaving us to wonder why he
behaved in that fashion. If we were near
enough closely to observe his movements
and the expression of his face, we may be able
to guess the reason of his behaviour ; but we
shall not be sure that we have the correct
explanation, until we can hear his own account

of the incident. Then, perhaps, he tells us that he went to get a drink, or that he heard " such a funny noise " in the house, that he saw approaching a savage dog or some person whom he dislikes, or that he was stung by a wasp, that he suddenly remembered it was time for school, that he heard his mother calling, or that he had just thought out a plan for making a kite. Any one of these statements would probably satisfy our curiosity ; and we should feel that we understood this particular piece of behaviour. For under similar circumstances we have behaved in similar fashion, and we have observed other persons so behave. But it is clear that any such explanation is only proximate and superficial, and that our understanding of the behaviour is only very partial. Such superficial explanation and such partial understanding are all that we can achieve without bringing psychology to our aid, that is to say, without applying to this particular instance the general principles of behaviour which systematic study has established.

Note first that the boy's explanation of his behaviour is given in words which partially describe his state of consciousness and which enable us to achieve by sympathetic understanding, in the light of our own experience of similar situations, a fuller description of that state than his words actually convey. If he, for example, mentions the drink, the "funny noise," or the savage dog, we know that he felt thirst, or curiosity, or fear. Such reconstruction in imagination of the state of consciousness of the individual is always the first step towards that completer understanding of behaviour of any kind which will enable us to control or modify either our own behaviour or that of others.

And this is true not only of human behaviour, but of all behaviour. If we see a mouse or other small animal dart back into its hole, we achieve a partial explanation and understanding of its behaviour, when we are able to infer that it felt frightened, or that it heard the cry of its little ones. Although, then, understanding of this kind is more incomplete and problematic the more unlike ourselves is the creature whose behaviour we observe, the explanation of the behaviour of any creature must always involve the description of its consciousness at the time. Now in order to describe any event or process, we are compelled by the nature of our intellect to analyse it into parts, each of which we conceive as an example of a class which we mentally fix or grasp by the use of a name. Thus, even such a simple process as the flight of a stone thrown from the hand can only be described by analysing its path into a series of positions occupied by it at successive moments of time, and then stating that its flight consists in its successively occupying these positions. And our observation of any event will be more complete and adequate, the more adequate are the notions of its several components that we form by the aid of language.

Now, when we come to describe the facts of consciousness, we find that the notions and the words in popular use are very inadequate to the work of analytic description. The first task of the student of psychology, the presupposition of all other psychological investigation, is therefore to refine, by the aid of the terminology and the descriptions made by his predecessors, his power of distinguishing, classifying, and describing the constituent features of the stream of his own consciousness. The observation or noticing of his own consciousness is what is called introspection. Introspection has been made something of a mystery. It is sometimes written of as though it were a feat which only a specially trained acrobat could perform. There has been much learned discussion as to whether it is possible, how it is possible, and how it is actually carried out. But, like many other things we do, we can do it very well without being able to say exactly how we do it. Every intelligent person can and frequently does give some description of his consciousness ; as when he says that he hears a sound, or that he has a toothache, describing perhaps its peculiar quality ; or when he says that he feels warm, or pleased, or tired, or angry, or doubtful, or confused, or sad ; or that he is thinking of something, or longing for it, or trying hard to recollect a name, or comparing any two things, or trying to make up his mind. All these and a hundred other current phrases we commonly use when we wish to make others aware of the state of our consciousness. And the introspection and analytic description of the psychologist involve merely the refinement of observation and description of this common kind, which we all habitually practise in various degrees.

The acquisition of familiarity with the current descriptive terms and with the classification of the things denoted by these terms must be the student's first step in taking up any science ; and it must go hand in hand with the repeated observation and examination of the things or processes described. The use of the current terms (in so far as they are well chosen) enables us to observe more fully and accurately ; for each name serves to fix our attention upon some particular feature or phase of the complex object of our observation, and thus, by fixing our attention in turn upon its several principal features, helps us to analyse the whole into its constituent parts. And the observations we make render our understanding of the terms fuller, and our use of them more accurate. Thus, when on beginning the study of botany the student takes a flower in his hand, he can observe it, and describe it in a rough way, distinguishing its most prominent features by the aid of ill-defined terms of popular speech. He then learns to apply to each of its parts its scientific name, petal, sepal, pistil, stamen, and so forth ; and as he repeats this double process of observation and naming on the variety of flowers, his power of observation and his usage of the scientific terminology improve hand in hand; and both improvements are due to the fact that his thought of a flower, which at first was confused and vague, has become more definite and richer in meaning ; he has learnt to know the parts in detail, and to know the whole as the sum of the parts related according to a definite plan.

The work of the beginner in psychology is of just the same nature. He finds himself able to observe his mental processes and to describe them in a vague confused manner by the aid of common language ; and his first step must be to refine his powers of observation and description by adopting the names provided by his predecessors and the distinctions implied by them. In doing this, he will find that his thought of any mental process becomes more definite and richer in meaning ; instead of thinking of it as a confused indeterminate whole, he thinks of it as a whole of a particular kind, comprising many parts related to one another according to a more or less definite system.

But, though this first step in psychology is essentially similar to the first step in any other concrete science, namely, a process of improvement of one's acquaintance with certain objects by means of analytic observation and description, it must be frankly recognized that this first step in psychology is of peculiar difficulty. In studying a flower, or any physical object such as a piece of rock, or an engine, or even a political system, the teacher may point to and name each part in turn, saying—There is a petal, there a stamen, there an anther, and so on. But in studying consciousness this direct designation is impossible ; the teacher can only describe the conditions under which certain modes of consciousness will in all probability be experienced ; he cannot point to a feeling of pain or of fear and say—That is a pain, or a fear. He can only say—Pain is what you would probably feel if your best friend cut you dead ; or—Fear is what you would feel if a savage dog suddenly attacked you. But men are so widely different that they react to similar situations in very different ways, and one can never be sure that the situation given or described will evoke the same mental reaction in any two persons. The situation that evokes pain or fear in one man may provoke another to anger, and leave a third unmoved.

Secondly, analytic observation of mental processes is difficult just because they are processes and not fixed enduring objects. We cannot examine at leisure and again and again the same mental process ; for, as we try to notice its peculiar quality and complexity, it changes every moment, and it can never be perfectly recovered or restored ; and it changes, or rather gives place to another process, all the more quickly, just because we direct our attention to it.

Beside these intrinsic difficulties, stands a third great difficulty which arises from the backward or rudimentary state of the science, the difficulty, namely, that the greatest authorities have not yet learnt to use the same descriptive terms, or to supply the same terms in exactly the same senses. It results from this lack of agreement among writers on psychology that, even in respect of this preliminary work, the description of consciousness, the beginner is apt to become greatly confused on turning from one author to another. It is important that he should not attach undue importance to these differences of descriptive method ; he should realize that each method may be legitimate and useful. He must recognize that any description we can give is necessarily inadequate and inevitably distorts the facts in some degree ; and he must aim at choosing for his own use the method that seems to be most effective.

The method of description most commonly used is what may be called the " cinematographic " or " static " method. One's consciousness is always complex and always changing ; it is the progressive manifestation of an unceasing activity, which activity is only partially revealed to us as consciousness. Now the cinematographic method of description abstracts from, or neglects, this active aspect of consciousness, and attempts to describe each phase of it as it is or subsists, without reference to the functions subserved by it.

Consciousness may be likened to the surface of a spring of water which bubbles up unceasingly from obscure invisible sources. The surface assumes at every moment new forms ;

some change rapidly, others slowly, but none persists stably ; each detail of the form of the surface is constantly giving place to new ones, some slowly, others more rapidly. The complexity and the rapidity of change are so great that it is impossible for the mind to seize all the details of any one moment, much less to observe just how each detail changes. The cinematographic method, therefore, begins by giving names to the principal varieties of the forms that present themselves ; it then attempts to describe the whole surface as it exists at any moment, by enumerating the forms presented by it at that moment ; and it attempts to represent the actual course of the changes of the whole surface by describing in such general terms its appearance at successive moments. That is to say, it analyses the perpetual flux into a complex of elements each statically conceived, and it describes the flux as consisting in the simultaneous and successive appearances of these elements. It is as though each of the successive pictures of a cinematograph film were first constructed by painting in by hand the various objects in the positions occupied by them at the moment represented by the picture.

Now, besides abstracting from the active or functional aspect of consciousness, this method necessarily falsifies the facts by neg-

lecting the actual changes and by breaking
up the continuity of the whole stream of
consciousness, both the continuity of the parts
which make up the whole at any one moment
of time and the continuity of the whole at
successive moments. Nevertheless, owing to
the nature of our intellects, this is the only
method by aid of which we can approximate
to a full and detailed description of the stream
of consciousness. It is, therefore, a valuable
and, perhaps, indispensable method. But
we must beware of being misled by it into
regarding the phases and details which we
mentally fix by the aid of names as things
that endure or persist as self-identical entities.
For to do this is the natural tendency of our
minds, to which many writers have yielded,
with the result that they have come to regard
consciousness as a mosaic of particles or
elements of consciousness, juxtaposed in ever-
changing combinations : that is to say, having
mentally analysed the continuous flux of
consciousness, by directing attention in turn
to a number of its most prominent features,
they think of it as though they had actually
broken it up into a number of separately
existing parts, and as though it were capable
of being reconstructed by bringing these parts
together again in simultaneous and successive
series.

If this method of description is to be used, we must have some general name for the features that we distinguish within the stream of consciousness ; and perhaps the best word for this purpose is " feeling " ; for this word commits us to no theory or presupposition. Adopting it, we may say that the stream of consciousness, considered in itself and apart from its functions, may be analytically resolved into a complex of feelings.

A word which has been more commonly used for this purpose is " idea." But most of those who have used this word have yielded themselves up unresistingly to the tendency to " reify " these abstractions, i.e. to treat ideas as things endowed with intrinsic properties and forces ; and the whole of mental life has been represented as the interplay of these things, the ideas. For these reasons it is well to avoid the use of the word " idea " ; though it must be confessed that the usage is so very convenient and so much in accordance with our natural tendency to reify, or regard as a thing, whatever our attention is directed to by the use of a name, that we can hardly hope to supersede it completely and at once.

A more modern fashion is to describe consciousness as a stream of sensations. Now the use of the word " sensation " has the same misleading tendency as that of the word " idea " ;

namely, it tempts us to regard consciousness as made up by the juxtaposition of things called sensations. Nevertheless, the notion and the word are so useful that we can hardly hope to describe consciousness without their aid ; and we must therefore accept that aid, while guarding ourselves carefully against the abuse of it. If we try to define what we mean by sensation, we must first recognize that the sensations, or sensory elements, which, according to the cinematographic method of description, make up so large a part of consciousness, are of two classes, the vivid and the faint. The vivid sensation can only be defined as the feeling which regularly follows upon the stimulation of a sense-organ. It is a fact of common experience, which has been confirmed and studied in detail by scientific experiment, that, whenever a physical impression of a particular kind is applied to a particular sense organ, there follows immediately a feeling of a particular quality. We are capable of experiencing a large variety of such sensations or feeling-qualities determined by stimulation of the senses ; and each such quality of feeling may be experienced in various degrees of intensity, which form a continuous series. Thus, whenever a tuning-fork of a given pitch is sounded in my neighbourhood, the air waves set up by its vibrations impinge on my ear and there stimulate the auditory nerve, with the result that I experience a sensation of tone of a particular quality ; and this sensation, or feeling-quality, is more or less intense according to the amplitude of the air waves that impinge on my ear, while its quality depends upon the rate of succession of the vibrations.

The sensory feelings of the second class, the faint sensations, or " sensory images " as they are now more commonly called, can only be defined by reference to the former class of vivid sensations. If, when the tuning-fork has ceased to vibrate, I think of its tone, I experience again the same quality of feeling ; but, though the feeling has the same quality as the vivid sensation, it differs from it in a way which we indicate by the term " faint." The difference between the vivid sensation and the image or faint sensation of the same quality is not of the same order as that between an intense and a less intense sensation of the same quality ; it is rather a difference of an altogether peculiar or unique kind. I experience many other sensation qualities, though not all, in this peculiar faint form. And the same seems to be true of all other persons ; though some experience predominantly images of one or more senses, and others those of other senses.

One influential school of psychologists, the " sensational " school, holds that the consciousness of any person may be completely described in terms of such sensations and images. But others hold that we must distinguish feelings of radically different kinds or orders ; some would recognize a class of affective feelings, of which the types are pleasure and pain ; and, while some admit these as the only two feeling qualities of this order, others recognize a larger variety of affective feelings. Others again recognize a third kind or order of feeling qualities, namely, the feelings of effort or activity ; and here again, while some recognize only one quality of this order, others recognize a variety of such feelings, each of specific and irreducible quality.

Now this method of regarding and describing consciousness is indispensable for certain purposes, for example, when we study the nervous conditions of the various qualities and intensities of sensation ; but as the result of thoroughgoing attempts to describe consciousness exhaustively in this way, it is becoming generally recognized that an exhaustive description in such terms is impossible. For over and above all the features that are capable of being introspectively seized and described in general terms as sensations or other feelings of specific qualities, the consciousness of any moment involves something more subtle which eludes all attempts to describe it in this way. And this residue, though it is so subtle and elusive, is nevertheless the most important part of consciousness. It is the essential thought-activity ; it is the reference of consciousness to an object ; and it can only be defined or described by naming the object of which the subject is thinking at the moment. If we wish to describe it statically, we can only do so by saying that it is the " meaning " which is present to consciousness. All the sensory feelings are but the medium which brings this thought-activity into play and determines its direction from moment to moment ; they are but solicitations to thought or to thinking.

We can best realize the truth of this statement by reflecting on such experiences as the following. As I lie in deep sleep, some one knocks on the door of my room and repeats his knock at short intervals of time, bringing me at each repetition a step nearer to the fully waking state. On looking back on this experience, it seems that I first heard the sound in an extremely obscure and imperfect manner, which I am tempted to describe by saying that my consciousness consisted merely of the sensation of sound ; that on repetition

of the knock, I again experienced a similar
sensation, but that, in addition to this, I
vaguely apprehended the sound as such, as
something there ; or, in other words, the impression of sound was no longer a bare sensation, but evoked a vague meaning, an act of
knowing or cognition ; that on further repetition of the knock, the impression of sound
evoked a richer and more definite meaning,
the cognitive activity became fuller and more
effective, and I recognized the sound as a
knock upon the door.

Similar experiences of other senses may be
cited to illustrate the same fact. In turning
over the pages of a book, I may come upon
a picture which at first glance appears to me as
merely a confused blur of colour patches. I
continue to look at it, and presently I resolve
the patches of colour into the parts of some
object or scene of a familiar type. The sense-
impression, which at first was nothing more
than a field of colour, evokes at a later moment
a definite meaning, a thought-activity in the
form of a cognition of a group of objects in
definite relations to one another. In such
cases the meaning, which, as we say, we read
into the sense-impression, suddenly appears
as an enrichment of consciousness over and
above the mere subsistence of the field of
sensations.

But we need not go to exceptional experiences to illustrate the fact. At every moment of my waking life, my various sense-organs are receiving physical impressions from a variety of objects ; rays of light from many objects are entering my eye, forming optical images upon my retina, and stimulating my optic nerve ; sounds from many sources are assailing my ears, contacts and odours my skin and nose. And all these sense-impressions affect my consciousness in the way of exciting sensations. But of all the objects which are thus exciting sensations at any moment, I am clearly aware of perhaps one only, or, if I am sunk in reflective thought, of none of them. When my attention is given to any one of these objects, the sensations excited by it initiate a process of mental activity ; they evoke a meaning, and I apprehend the object as such or such. All the rest of the sensations present in consciousness remain obscure and meaningless, or almost so ; they are said to constitute the margin of the field of consciousness, while the object singled out for attentive scrutiny is said to occupy the centre of that field.

It is the marginal sensations which are most difficult to describe by any other than the cinematograph method. No doubt they play some slight part in determining the course

of mental activity ; but their functional relation to this activity is so obscure that it
eludes us, and we can only describe them by
saying that they subsist as sensations making
up together this margin of the field of consciousness. It may be said with some plausibility that all of the sense-impressions received
by our organs solicit our attention. Each
one, probably, tends, and tends more strongly
the more intense it is, to determine the
direction of our mental activity ; but if so,
then only some few can at any one moment
play an effective part of this sort and be taken
up into the main current of consciousness.

The consciousness of any person always
involves, then, not only a more or less complex
mass of feelings, but also this thought-activity
which cannot be described by the cinematograph method. The proportions of the two
constituents of consciousness vary widely ;
during abstract thinking, the feeling mass may
be relatively slight, consisting of little more
than a train of images of words heard or seen,
while a rich stream of meanings passes through
consciousness. On the other hand, when the
mind is inactive, when it approaches the
condition of sleep or of complete confusion,
the thought-activity is very slight, while the
feeling-mass may be large. Thus, as I lie
just awaking from deep dreamless sleep, my

sense-organs may be assailed by many strong impressions which evoke a complex mass of feelings of high intensity, but nevertheless I may remain for some moments mentally inactive ; the sounds, or sights, or smells, or touches, that assail me have no meaning for me, or but a minimum of meaning.   Whether it is possible for any one's thought-activity to be reduced to zero, while feeling still continues, is a theoretical question, to which it seems impossible to return a definite answer ; for, if any one were reduced to that state, he would be incapable of describing it, or of remembering it on returning to a more active or fully waking condition.   This hypothetical state of mind has been called one of anoetic sentience or thoughtless feeling.   With the possible exception of such states of anoetic sentience, to be conscious is to be mentally active.

To speak, then, of consciousness and to attempt to describe consciousness as something that exists and can be analysed into constituent parts which severally exist, abstracting from or neglecting the mental activity or function, is to distort the facts very seriously and to use a method which cannot be wholly successful.   This method of description is useful for certain special purposes ; but, when we set out to gain insight into mental process in general, we shall do better to follow a method of description which does less violence to the facts.

Now, when we regard consciousness as an activity, we cannot ignore the fundamental fact that some one is conscious, the fact that I am conscious, or that some other organism more or less like myself is conscious ; that is to say, consciousness does not exist of itself, but is an activity of some being which, in all cases of which we have positive knowledge, is a material organism, but to which we may conveniently give the general name, *subject*.

A second fundamental fact is that to be conscious is to be conscious of something ; which thing is properly called the *object* of my consciousness. Being conscious is, then, an activity of a *subject* in relation to an *object* ; and we shall do well to choose as our most general term for describing the facts a verb, rather than a substantive such as consciousness. The best verb for this purpose is the verb *to think of*. The word *think* is used by some authors to refer only to mental processes of the higher or more intellectual kind ; but it may be used with advantage in this wider and more general sense, in which it is equivalent to the clumsy expression *to be conscious of*.

Whenever, then, there is mental activity,

some subject is thinking of some object ; the object may be a material thing, or a physical process, or a mental activity, or an abstract quality or property, such as virtue, or weight, or heat, or any other object which we can distinguish or to which we can direct our attention and discourse. In the typical act of thinking we can distinguish three aspects ; the subject knows the object as such or such, he is pleasurably or painfully affected by it, and he strives to bring about some change in it or in his relation to it. It is generally maintained that every mental act presents these three aspects ; or is at once a knowing, a being affected, and a striving ; or, in technical terms, a cognition, an affection (or a feeling in the narrower sense of this word), and a conation. For example, on looking at a flower, I apprehend or cognize or know it as a flower of a particular shape and colour, I am pleased by it, and I examine it more closely in order to know it more fully.

These are not separable parts of the thinking process ; nevertheless, we must regard the affection and the striving as consequential upon the knowing, and the character of the striving as in some degree determined by the affection ; but in turn the striving reacts upon the knowing, maintains and furthers it, and

leads to modification of the feeling.   And so
the cycle continues and the thinking progresses towards its natural end, which is the
satisfaction brought by the terminal cognition.
To illustrate again by the case of the flower ;
the initial apprehension of its colour pleases
me and stimulates me to examine it more
closely, with the more or less explicit purpose
of discovering its botanical position ; the
closer examination, maintained and governed
by this purpose, enables me to know it more
fully ; and the whole cycle of activity comes
to its natural end when I have seized the
distinguishing features of the flower and
recognized it as a variety of this or that species
and genus.   Mental activity or thinking thus
tends to progress in cycles ; each cycle begins
with knowing, which excites feeling and striving ; the striving results in a new knowing,
which satisfies the striving ; and so the cycle
reaches its natural termination in a feeling of
satisfaction.   By adopting this method of
describing mental process, we may hope to
avoid the falsifications of the facts which the
cinematograph method tends so strongly to
produce ; especially the abstraction from both
subject and object ; the " reification " of the
steps of mental activity ; and the ignoring
of the essentially purposive character of the
process.   If for certain purposes of detailed

description we make use of that method, we shall keep it in complete subordination to the truer method, remaining fully aware of the distortion of the facts produced by it.   In this way we may hope to combine the advantages and to avoid the drawbacks of both methods.

The two methods and the combination of them may be illustrated by the description of an imperfect recollection of a particular flower previously seen on a single occasion. The description according to the thorough-going cinematograph method would run as follows : My idea of the flower consists of visual images which are imperfect reproductions of the sensations that composed my percept of it.   The truer method would be to say—I think of the flower in visual terms, but I cannot faithfully reproduce in memory the colours of its various parts as they appeared to me when I perceived it.   The convenient combined method would be to say—I recollect the flower in visual terms, but my colour-images do not faithfully reproduce the colour-sensations.

If every mental process is at once a knowing, an affection, and a striving, it must be recognized that one or other of these aspects is commonly dominant ; so that we are led to speak of each kind of mental process by the name of the dominant aspect ; thus we speak of acts of perception, recognition, recollection, reasoning, when we are predominantly cognitive ; of states of emotion, or feeling, when affection is dominant ; of volition, resolution, deciding, desiring, when we are vividly conscious of striving towards an end. It is this way of speaking which has led to the common error of regarding these aspects of all mental process as separable functions ; an error of which the commonest and most serious form has been to regard intellectual processes as capable of being purely cognitive or completely freed from the influence of the emotions and the will.

We pass on to observe that, though the devising of an appropriate method of describing consciousness is an important and difficult task which has not yet been completed, yet such description is merely a first step in the study of behaviour. In itself a mere description of the consciousness of any subject does nothing to explain his behaviour. It is true that in many cases a man's behaviour is in large measure explained by even a very partial description of his consciousness at the time ; but this is only in virtue of our knowledge of certain laws or rules of the connexion between certain modes of consciousness and certain modes of behaviour which experience has led us to formulate, however roughly and vaguely. Thus, if I call on a friend and find him walking rapidly up and down his room, gesticulating wildly and muttering incoherently, I may feel that his behaviour is explained, in a partial or proximate fashion at least, when he tells me that he is filled with rage, or grief, or remorse ; for, through various experiences of my own as well as through the observation of others, I have learnt that each of these emotions is commonly accompanied by, or expresses itself in, a peculiar mode of behaviour. One task of psychology is, then, to refine and correct these empirical generalizations in which we all formulate more or less explicitly the relations of concomitance between modes of behaviour and modes of consciousness or thinking.

But my friend's statement that he is filled with anger, or grief, or remorse, is at best but a very partial explanation of his behaviour ; before I can feel that I have an adequate explanation, I require to know what made him angry, or grieved, or remorseful. Consider a more complicated case. Suppose I am told the bare fact that an acquaintance of mine has shot and killed a man. Being utterly at a loss to understand this behaviour, I go to him and seek to find the explanation. In doing this I am forestalling the judge and jury ; for when

c

the homicide is brought before them, their business precisely is to discover the psychological explanation of the behaviour which resulted in homicide ; and, according to the nature of the psychological conclusion they reach, they will bring in a verdict of accidental homicide, of justifiable homicide, of wilful and malicious murder, or of wilful murder with extenuating circumstances, or of homicide due to insane delusions, or of homicide during a paroxysmal mental derangement ; and the treatment meted out to the offender will be determined by the nature of this purely psychological verdict. I dwell upon the legal aspect of our imaginary case, because it will serve to bring home to the reader in a forcible manner the fact, so constantly ignored, that none of us can escape the necessity of frequently making psychological judgments, and that our relations with our fellows are determined at every point by such judgments. It is true that we attempt to simplify, or to avoid altogether, the exercise of psychological judgment, by accepting and applying a number of moral maxims or formulæ, such as—to kill, or to steal, or to lie, is wrong—to forgive injury, or to relieve distress, or to repress anger, is right. But only the most thoughtless of men can be content to apply these maxims to the acts of his fellows without reference to the motives or the mental processes of which their acts are the issues. Now, as soon as one inquires after motives of behaviour, one enters upon a psychological problem and requires all the help that psychology can give ; just as surely as the man who sets out to build an aeroplane enters upon a mechanical problem and requires all the help that the science of mechanics can afford.

To go back now to our acquaintance, Jonson, who has been so unfortunate as to kill a man, Smith. If we learn that Jonson struck down his victim in a fit of fury, we know that the act was not accidental, but was in some sense purposive : but, before we can understand or pass any moral judgment upon the act, we must know the conditions that excited this violent emotion. We may learn that Smith was a casual stranger who, in the course of an altercation with Jonson, had struck him or used grossly insulting language ; or that Smith had perpetrated a gross outrage upon the dearest object of Jonson's affections ; or that Smith had long used a position of advantage over Jonson to torment him and injure him, in a spirit of wanton cruelty ; or that Jonson, after repeatedly failing in various undertakings, had gradually become moody and suspicious, frequently resenting the actions of perfectly innocent persons whom

he believed to be scheming to injure him ; or
that Jonson had furiously assaulted Smith,
just after recovering from an epileptic fit, and
seems to remember nothing of the incident.   In
the last case we recognize that the information
enables us to class the act in the category
of post-epileptic paroxysms, of which we can
say little more than that such paroxysms of
fury have been observed to follow upon
epileptic attacks, and that they imply a grave
disorder of the constitution of the organism.
In each of the other cases the nature of the
train of mental activity leading up to the
action is indicated in a general way, and the
action is in so far explained.   But it is rendered
intelligible to us only in virtue of the fact that
we have a general knowledge of human nature
and of the way in which it is liable to react
to special circumstances.   Each phase of the
mental processes and of the behaviour which
led up to the final catastrophe was a reaction
of human nature to particular circumstances.
If we have no intimate acquaintance with
Jonson, we can carry our explanation no
further : we have to be content with recognizing that each particular mode of reaction
to the circumstances described was such as
the constitution of men in general renders
possible.   But, if we are intimately acquainted
with Jonson, we may be able to see that his

nature was such that, under the given circumstances, the state of consciousness and mode of behaviour evoked were just such as we might have anticipated.

These considerations will serve to bring home to us the truth of the following proposition ; namely, that psychology, the science of behaviour, cannot confine itself merely to describing consciousness as accurately and exhaustively as possible, nor to establishing, as empirical rules, the concurrence of certain conscious processes with certain forms of action or behaviour ; but that it must seek also to explain both the processes of consciousness and the associated modes of behaviour as the issue of certain enduring conditions which we speak of collectively as the constitution of the mind. This constitution is something that we cannot directly observe ; we can only infer it. Each of us can observe only his own consciousness and the behaviour of himself and of his fellow-creatures ; and he can receive from his fellow-men reports of their consciousness. From these data he has to construct by a process of imaginative inference an account, as serviceable as may be, of that hidden and extraordinarily complex thing which we call human nature, or the constitution of the human mind.

We are now in a position to make a proper

use of the word " mind." We may define the mind of any organism as the sum of the enduring conditions of its purposive activities. And, in order to mark our recognition of the fact that these conditions are not a mere aggregation, but form rather an organized system of which each part is functionally related to the rest in definite fashion, we may usefully speak of the " structure " of the mind. This structure of the mind is something which, although we cannot observe it, endures throughout the life of the individual ; and all mental and bodily activities are expressions and revelations of its nature. From the most general observation of the course of life of human beings, we can confidently infer that the structure of the mind develops gradually from birth onwards, increasing in complexity and definiteness of organization up to a certain period of life, and then, if life is prolonged, gradually undergoing some regressive changes. We can confidently infer also that the course of its development is governed in two ways, partly by an intrinsic tendency to develop along certain lines which are determined by the ancestry or heredity of the individual ; partly by the influences of the environment, which promote in very diverse degrees the actualization of the various hereditary potentialities.

CHAPTER III

THE STRUCTURE OF THE MIND

In what terms shall we describe the structure of the mind? How are we to conceive it? This is a question of fundamental importance for psychology; but no one answer to it has yet secured general acceptance.

Let us glance at some of the principal ways in which this problem has been dealt with. An old-fashioned method of dealing with it is to describe the mind as consisting of a bundle of faculties, assigning each of the mental functions that is commonly distinguished and named to a faculty of the same name; such as the faculties of perception, conception, imagination, judgment, reason, will, and, related to all these in some utterly obscure fashion, the faculty of memory. This doctrine is one of great importance; for its great simplicity has recommended it to the general mind, and it still forms the implicit basis of much of the current educational theory and practice. Our schoolboys are set to geometry, in order to develop the faculty of reason; to learning by heart poetry and dates and irregular verbs, in order to develop the faculty of memory; to composing Latin verses, in order to develop the faculty of taste; and so on, and so on; and though the "faculty psychology" has long been regarded as out of date, the wisdom of these practical applications of it has been seriously and effectively challenged in recent years only.

Another way of describing the structure of the mind which has enjoyed a great vogue, was devised in association with the method of describing mental activity as a sequence of ideas. Every idea was regarded as capable of existing in two conditions or forms : on the one hand, it might be a conscious idea or exist in consciousness, consciousness being spoken of as an illuminated chamber into which ideas enter in turn, to be lit up and active for a short period ; and on the other hand, it might exist as an unconscious idea in the memory, a sort of Hades or dim underworld to which each idea, or its ghost, returns after its brief exposure to the light of consciousness ; there to await and to seize any opportunity of emerging again into light and life. Within this underworld ideas remain linked together in complex groupings. The whole assembly of ideas, thus linked in the obscurity of memory, constitutes the structure of the mind ; and mental activity consists in each idea dragging up after it into the light whatever ideas are linked or associated with it.

Another way of conceiving what we have called the structure of the mind is to identify it with the structure of the nervous system. This method has commonly been adopted by those who accept literally the description of consciousness as an agglomeration of sensations. Each sensation is regarded as attached to some functional element of the nervous system or brain. These brain-elements are conceived as connected together to form an immensely complex machine. Physical impressions, falling upon parts of this machine, set free in it currents of energy, which run hither and thither in a manner determined by the connexions of the parts, and, finding exit in the motor nerves that actuate the muscles, bring about all the bodily movements that make up behaviour ; and certain of the brain-elements, when thus stirred up to play their parts as links of the mechanism, as cogs of the machine, throw off incidentally sensations of various qualities ; the successive conjunctions of which constitute the stream of consciousness. Some such view as this is very widely accepted, and, actuated by a belief in its literal truth, thousands of busy workers, who turn aside from psychology as from a mystical study comparable to astrology or alchemy, are devoting their lives to the minute exploration of the structure of the brain with scalpel and microscope and a hundred ingenious methods of refined re-

search, convinced that therein lies the secret
of human nature.

Now we have admitted already the possibility that this view and this method may
ultimately justify themselves ; but there are
three good reasons why we should not adopt
them in the present state of science. First,
we have no warrant for the assumption that
the mechanical processes of material structures,
however complex, can issue in movements
that have the characteristics of behaviour.
Secondly, we have no warrant for believing
that such processes can of themselves produce
sensations or feeling of any kind, or can be
in any sense identified with the processes of
consciousness. Thirdly, if we adopted this
view, we should hamper ourselves by laying
down fixed limits within which our thought
must move, when we set out to build up our
conception of the structure of the mind.
Of course, if the view were well established,
this restriction of the range of speculation
would be purely advantageous ; but, so long
as the whole problem remains obscure, we
ought to avoid the acceptance of such limits ;
for it may well be that this structure is quite
incapable of being adequately described in
terms of the spatial distribution of elements
of any kind.

Here a word of warning must be given

against the tendency, so natural to most of us, to think of all structure after the pattern of material structures ; that is, as consisting in a spatial arrangement of connected parts. It seems worth while to point out that common usage approves the use of the word " structure " to describe systems which have nothing of this nature. We speak of the structure of a story, or of a play, or of a piece of music ; meaning thereby that, when we contemplate the whole, we see that it consists of parts each of which is related to the whole and to all the other parts in a fashion which is significant for, or contributes to determine the characteristic nature of, the whole. It is in this sense, of a whole consisting of systematically related parts, that we speak of the structure of the mind. But we must not assume that the structure of a play or of a sonata provides a perfect analogy for the structure of the mind ; although the analogy may be closer than that furnished by the structure of a steam engine.

We have, then, to build up our notion of the structure of the mind by an intricate process of creative imagination, inferring its nature from our observation of the operations it achieves, which operations are only partially revealed to us on introspection and in the behaviour of living things.

We have rejected as unsatisfactory three of the traditional methods of describing the structure of the mind. But in rejecting these, we should endeavour to hold fast to whatever of truth they have revealed ; for it is highly improbable that methods accepted and used by many able men have proved altogether barren ; and the best way to arrive at a better method is to try to remedy the deficiencies of these traditional methods by combining their meritorious features.

Now, the most effective of these older methods was, undoubtedly, that which described mental process as consisting in the succession of ideas, and the structure of the mind as consisting in the system of latent ideas. The exponents of this method have generally claimed for it as a great merit that it enables us to dispense with the notion of faculties ; yet one of its weaknesses is indicated by the fact, that many of those who have attempted to work by it have combined it in some degree with the method of faculties. They have spoken of the mind as exercising its faculties upon or about its ideas, as comparing them, recalling them, combining or distinguishing them, holding fast or rejecting them, or as otherwise reacting or operating upon them. This tendency results from the inherent impossibility of describing mental process by the cinematograph method, and of ignoring the agency or activity of a subject. We cannot, in fact, get rid of the notion of the subject by substituting for it a collection or system of ideas ; the subject is, at least, that which has and enjoys the ideas and holds them together to form one mind. For, if we recognize ideas at all, we must also recognize that ideas considered as things are not scattered about the world as loose and separate existences, but that they cohere in systems, each of which constitutes a mind.

We have already approved of the method of describing mental process which consists in speaking of it as the activity of a subject ; but, instead of saying that the subject exercises these activities about ideas, we agreed to say that the subject, or (as we may now say if we prefer the mode of expression) the mind, thinks of objects in these various ways. Now, if we recognize a subject, we must admit that it has certain faculties ; for a subject devoid of capacities would be a nonentity. And by a " faculty " we mean a capacity for an ultimate, irreducible, or unanalysable mode of thinking of, or of being conscious of, objects ; a capacity which we have to accept as a fact, and which we cannot hope to explain as a conjunction of more fundamental capacities. In this sense, knowing, feeling and striving, must be recognized as faculties of the mind ; and we have to raise in regard to each one of them the question—Is it a single faculty, or is it a class of faculties of similar nature ? It seems necessary to accept the latter view. Striving seems to be of two ultimate kinds, namely, striving towards and striving away from the object, or appetition and aversion. Feeling or affection, again, seems to be of at least two ultimate kinds, namely, agreeable and disagreeable feeling, or pleasure and displeasure. There seems good reason also to recognize feeling of excitement and feeling of depression as equally ultimate and irresolvable, and, therefore, as faculties of the subject. It is difficult to see how we can refuse to admit a larger variety of faculties of feeling. Our emotions are infinitely various ; but most of them seem capable of being analysed and exhibited as conjunctions of a small number of primary emotions ; each of these seems to be a mode of feeling which is not capable of further analysis, and which is, therefore, an ultimate mode of being conscious that implies a corresponding faculty. But this is a very difficult question ; and in respect to it we must keep open minds.

Now we have to face the question—Is knowing the exercise of a single faculty, or must we recognize a variety of modes of knowing, each being the exercise of a distinct faculty? In attempting to answer this question, we must observe the following principles : whatever in our thinking can be described in terms of the object does not imply a faculty ; a faculty is only implied by a mode of thinking of an object which is ultimate and irreducible ; a faculty may be exercised about objects of every kind. It would seem that we cannot be content to admit only one mode of knowing, namely, simple apprehension or awareness of objects. For besides simply thinking or being aware of objects, we affirm or deny them ; and these seem to be ultimate modes of knowing or thinking (or two varieties of one ultimate mode) : affirming and denying, then, seem to be rooted in a special faculty (or faculties), and all processes of judgment and reasoning seem to be instances of the exercise of this faculty.

It is hard to deny that the activity of comparing is the exercise of a special faculty ; but it is doubtful whether we ought to recognize any others ; for every mode of thinking other than those already named, can probably be explained as the conjoint exercise of the faculties enumerated above. To recognize, for example, or to remember, is to think of the same object again, and to judge or affirm it to be the same object that we thought of before. To perceive (in the strict

sense) is to think of an object as here at hand ;
but that which distinguishes perceiving from
imagining, or from thinking of an object not
now at hand, seems capable of being described
as a difference between the objects in the two
cases. The same is true of the difference
between what is called an abstract idea, or a
general idea, and a particular idea ; the first
means thinking of an abstract object ; the
second means thinking of a class of things ;
the third means thinking of a particular
thing. Again, it may be asked—Does our
thinking of space and extension imply a
faculty of spatial intuition, as is sometimes
maintained ? To this the answer seems to
be—Space and extension and position are
objects, or attributes of objects, rather than
modes of thinking. And if the same question
is asked as regards time and duration, a
similar answer must be made. Duration is
an attribute of objects, not a mode of thinking.

So much of truth, then, we have to concede
to the method or theory of faculties, and to
take over from it. What now of the method
of ideas ? The fact which, according to the
method of ideas, was called the presence of
an idea of a certain object in consciousness,
we prefer to describe by saying that the
subject is thinking of the object. How, then,
are we to describe the fact which, according

to that method, was called the presence of the idea in a latent state in the storehouse of memory ?   Now, we are able to infer from a multitude of facts that the capacity of any subject to think in any way of any given object implies a corresponding particular development in the structure of his mind. Any man can think of those things only of which he has learned to think ; and this learning to think of an object is a process of gradual building up of the capacity by successive efforts to think the object more adequately ; and that which endures between the successive acts of thinking of this object is a potentiality of thinking of it again.   This potentiality is what the method of ideas describes as the persistence of an idea in the memory.   Now this potentiality is not, like the faculty of thinking, a potentiality of thinking in general, but a potentiality of thinking of a specific object.   There is, then, in the structure of any mind something that endures as the ground of the potentiality of thinking of each specific object which can be thought of by that mind.   For this we need a neutral non-committal name.   We have agreed that it should not be called an unconscious or latent idea.   Perhaps the best term by which to describe it is *mental disposition* ; for it is that which disposes or enables the mind to think of or to exercise its faculties, cognitive, affective, and conative, upon a corresponding object.

Each developed mind comprises a large number of such dispositions, and the development of a mind consists largely in the building up of such dispositions. We may try to imagine a completely undeveloped mind as consisting of faculties without dispositions ; that would be a mind with everything to learn. But all minds of which we have any knowledge possess some dispositions, and the mind of every normal human adult possesses a vast number. The mind of a man is, in fact, a microcosm in which the world, in so far as he can be said to know it, is represented in detail, a disposition for every kind of object and every kind of relation of which he can think. If, for example, he can think of a horse, or a cube, or heat, or joy, or the causal relation, it is in virtue of the existence in his mind of a disposition corresponding to each of these objects.

The many dispositions of any mind do not merely exist side by side ; rather they must be conceived as functionally connected to form a vast and elaborately organized system ; and this system is the structure of the mind. The more perfectly organized the mind, the more fully are the objects which compose the world and the relations between them represented in the mind by the dispositions and their functional relations. The total system formed by all the cognitive dispositions of the mind constitutes what is commonly called the knowledge possessed by that mind.

A principal task of psychology is, then, to provide a general description of these dispositions and their functional relations, and to give some general account of their development and organization. On these problems the various departments of psychological inquiry seek to throw light in their several ways, of which something will be said in later pages. Here some of the general conclusions to which they point may be indicated.

We have to conceive the cognitive dispositions as linked together in minor systems, and these minor systems as linked in larger mental systems, and these again in still larger systems ; and so on, by many steps of superordination, until the whole multitude are linked in the one vast system.

The relation between the dispositions of any one system of the lowest order must be conceived not as a direct connexion, but rather as consisting in their common connexion with a disposition of a higher order corresponding to a more general object. For example, the dispositions through which I think of horse and dog respectively are connected with that of a more general object, mammal ; and this in turn is connected with that of the still more general object, vertebrate ; and this again with that of the still more general object, animal.

The relation between the more general and the more special disposition is such that the activity of the latter involves the activity of the former ; so that, for example, I cannot think of a horse without thinking of it also as a mammal, as a vertebrate, and as an animal, and as a solid material object. That I do think of it in this complex fashion, even in the act of casually perceiving a horse, is shown by the fact that, if the horse exhibited properties other than those implied by these general terms, if I saw it fly up in the air, or swim under water, or lay an egg, or felt it offer no resistance to my touch, my mental process would be jarred and disordered and I should be thrown into a state of confusion and astonishment : I should hesitate to regard the object as a horse. In short, in perceiving the object as a horse, I bring into play a large store of knowledge acquired by experience, i.e. by previous thinking about horses, and about animals in general and material things in general. This example will serve to show how very inadequately so simple a process as perceiving a horse is described by saying that there is evoked in my consciousness a certain field of sensations of particular qualities and spatial arrangement. The sense-impression merely initiates the thinking process. A young child on seeing a horse for the first time might receive a sense-impression very similar to mine; but his perceiving would be a vastly simpler process than mine, and the difference between the two is quite incapable of being described in terms of sensations. Yet even his perceiving would be much more than the mere reception of the sense-impression; he would perceive it as a moving solid thing out there; and, if he had previous experience of cows, he might perceive—or, in more technical language, apperceive—it as a cow, perhaps, giving it that name and otherwise behaving towards it as he had learnt to behave towards cows.

If we use the static method of description, we must say that what makes my perception of the horse so much fuller and so much more adequate as a guide to action than the child's perception, is not any greater wealth of sensations or imagery in my consciousness, but a richer " meaning " evoked by the similar sense-impression. This " meaning " is the expression in consciousness of the coming into activity of a vast system of dispositions, built up in my mind through my thinking since the time I was a young child.

This example will serve also to show how inadequately the method of ideas describes the facts ; for my thinking of the horse is not the bringing out into the light of consciousness of some entity that had been lying stored in some dark pigeon-hole of the mind ; it was rather an exercise of the faculty of knowing determined and directed by the activity of a complex system of mental dispositions. For note that, when I perceive, or in any way think of, a dog, a large part of the same system is active ; for I know it as a mammal, a verte-brate, an animal, a solid object, and so forth ; and it is only in so far as I know it as a dog-mammal, rather than a horse-mammal, that the dispositions at work are different.

Again, suppose that instead of perceiving merely a horse, or a dog, I perceive my dog, Jack. The impression has for me a still richer meaning ; it means all that the impres-sion of any other dog means ; but I think of him not merely as a representative of the species dog, and as all that is implied by that, but also as the dog who will come at my call, who will behave in this or that way under various circumstances : I expect of him all that I expect of dogs in general, and much more besides. And my behaviour towards him is quite special and peculiar ; if a stranger kicks him, I feel as bitter resentment as if he had kicked me ; if he admires him, I am gratified. All which shows that within my mental system " dog " there has been differentiated a special subordinate system, which is active in addition to the whole dog-system when I think of my dog, Jack.

The last remark leads us to consider the way in which systems and dispositions develop in the mind. No disposition is an altogether new creation ; every one arises rather as a specialization, within some pre-existing disposition ; and in this way, by the specialization within it of a number of minor dispositions, a disposition becomes a system of dispositions. And, when the constituent dispositions of such a system in turn become systems through the differentiation of new dispositions within them, the parent system becomes as it were a grandparent, and later by further similar steps a great-grandparent. The mental system may, then, be likened to a family the successive generations of which continue to live and work contemporaneously ; the dispositions are the individual members ; the work of each such member is supported by all members of preceding generations in the direct line of descent. Thus the disposition by

means of which I think of my dog was differentiated from that of dog in general,
this from that of animal in general; and
so on.

This is an over-simplified account of the
growth and relation of mental systems. If
the process of descent, or budding, were the
only way in which systems develop, we
should be justified in regarding all the dispositions of any mind as the lineal descend-
ants of some one original disposition; and
we might find an analogy for the structure
of the mind in a tree with its stem, branches,
and twigs, each twig being supported by all
parts of the tree of which it is the lineal
descendant by budding. And, if the whole
process of development occurred in the course
of the life-history of a single mind, we might
describe that mind in its primitive undeveloped
condition as consisting of a single disposition,
which would enable its possessor to think only
of a single most highly general object. The
thinking of such a mind in its cognitive aspect
would be represented by the words " there
is something " ; the nature of the object
remaining quite unspecified. To describe the
growth of the mind in this way would be far
truer than to describe it as proceeding in the
inverse way (as has often been done) ; namely,
as beginning with the detailed apprehension of

a number of discrete objects as unrelated particulars, and as proceeding by the subsequent classing together of those which are seen to resemble one another, or by the bringing together in the mind of the ideas of features in which they resemble one another, to form a more general idea.

The young child does not begin by clearly distinguishing this cat and that dog, and does not then proceed to combine the like features of all cats in a general idea and those of all dogs in another ; and he does not thereafter construct a still more general idea of four-footed beast or animal. Rather he begins by perceiving all cats and all dogs as moving things which he shrinks from in fear or strives to hug in his arms ; and from such experiences he learns to think vaguely of such moving things as different from inert things ; the disposition so formed then becomes differentiated, as he learns to distinguish cat from dog, and to think of other animals in the same way, as things that move and respond to his actions as his fellow human beings do. Commonly the child seems to come, like most savages, to think of animals as beings like himself, accepting each new variety he comes across as a member of the same class of beings. And only gradually does he learn to distinguish the various kinds as unlike himself in various degrees. For the developing mind does not achieve of itself the scientific classification of the animal kingdom; that is a product of the work of many minds, which, being embodied in language, can be used to direct the growth and differentiation of the system in each developing mind.

But this differentiation by acts of progressive discrimination is not the only process by which the structure of the mind develops. There occurs also a process of another kind, which is of extreme importance. This is the process of perception of similarity between objects. As regards the dispositions and systems concerned, it is a process which results in the conjunction of previously separate systems to form a single system. In terms of the analogy presented by the structure of a tree, we may say that one branch becomes joined with another, so that their twigs beyond the point of junction are supported by their conjoint strength.

As an example of such a process, take the case of a child who has grown up without learning to regard plants as living beings, but, nevertheless, has learnt to think of them as a distinct class of things. Suddenly it is borne in upon him that plants also, like the animals, are alive; at that moment two systems become conjoined in his mind, and thereafter form a single larger system; the living-being system apperceives the other, and incorporates it with itself. In terms of the analogy of the successive generations of a family, we may say that diverging stocks or lines of descent become blended now and again by intermarriage.

As an example of a slightly different mode of this process, we may take the young student of physics who, having learnt to think of gases and of liquids as very different states of matter, suddenly becomes aware of those points of similarity in virtue of which they are classed together as fluid matter. The two systems built up by his observation of gases and liquids respectively, become conjoined in a new system, the possession of which thereafter enables the subject to think of the properties common to liquids and gases in abstraction from, or to the neglect of, the properties in which they differ. Or again, a child is familiar with the eggs of animals and with the seeds of plants, but has never thought of their similarities, until, perhaps, he is led to do so by hearing the word *egg* applied to the seed of a plant, or the word *germ* applied to both eggs and seeds; after which the word *germ* is used by him to mean the properties common to both classes of objects. In such cases the developing mind

is guided by language to effect the synthetic
process which some other mind has previously
achieved as a process of independent discovery. The classical instance of original
apperception usually cited is Newton's discovery of the likeness between the motion of
the moon and that of falling bodies, and his
consequent thinking of all such processes as
examples of gravitation.

The process of apperceptive synthesis produces a simplification of the structure of the
mind and of the language which reflects it,
by which they are rendered more effective
instruments of thinking. It may be regarded
as a process by which the failures of the
process of differentiation are rectified. For,
if we imagine a mind developing from the
primitive condition we have postulated on
an earlier page (p. 88) by ideally perfect
processes of successive discrimination of
objects and corresponding differentiation of
dispositions, we shall see that it would not
require the synthetic fusion of systems, in
order to perfect its structure and to become
a true microcosm accurately reflecting the
whole world of objects and their relations.
We may illustrate this point by referring
again to the world of life. We may suppose
that such a mind would first think of every
living thing it encountered simply as such,

without discriminating varieties ; it would know them simply as possessing the properties common to all living things ; in this, exercising the fundamental property of reacting in the same way to things in so far as they are alike. We may suppose that it would then discriminate animals from plants ; and then the great classes of each kingdom ; and so step by step arrive at discrimination of species, varieties, and lastly, individual creatures, differentiating in the process the corresponding dispositions.

Such, we may suppose, might be the course of development of a pure and perfect intellect, if such a being were possible. But the actual growth of our minds is very different. Each human mind takes up its course of development from a point already far advanced and with certain strong tendencies to react to objects, not merely according to their intrinsic likenesses and differences, but according to the way in which objects subserve the practical needs of the organism in which the mind is embodied ; and throughout its development each mind comes to know objects in those aspects which affect these practical needs, rather than in those which, from a purely intellectual point of view, would appear to be their essential and distinguishing features. Hence the need for that process of synthesis of systems, by which are discovered the essential similarities of things previously thought of in complete separation, if we are to achieve the capacity of thinking things in any other way than that which immediately subserves practical needs.

In all these processes of development of the human mind, the use of language plays a very important part. In the process of differentiation of dispositions by discrimination, the name helps to preserve as a system the original disposition within which differentiation takes place. For the hearing of a name given to an object fulfils the same function as the sense-impression received from it; namely, it brings the corresponding disposition into activity, and thus enables us to continue to conceive as a whole the class within which we have distinguished kinds or individuals; whereas, in the absence of the class-name, so soon as we had learnt to react differently to the objects we discriminate, we should cease to think of the class, the original object of higher generality, and the original disposition would decay. Thus a child, having through contact with various dogs learnt to think of the object dog-in-general, goes on to discriminate collie dogs and terriers, the two breeds most commonly represented in his neighbourhood; and we may suppose that his attitude to the two breeds is very different owing to the friendliness of the collies and the snappishness of the terriers. In these circumstances a child deprived altogether of the use of language would sharply distinguish the two classes and would tend to forget, that is, to lose the power of thinking of, dog-in-general. But a child who has first learnt to give the name dog to dogs of both breeds, will continue to think of this more general object on hearing the word *dog*, after discriminating collies and terriers. In a similar way a child brought up in the Southern States of the American Union learns first to think of man-in-general ; but later he learns to discriminate white men and " niggers " ; and their differences become so accentuated and their similarities so neglected, that, but for his command of the word *man*, he would be in danger of forgetting that black men and white men are varieties of the one species, Man, and of losing the power of thinking of the more general object, Man.

In relation to apperceptive synthesis language plays an even more important rôle. There has been much discussion of the question—Is thinking possible without language ? The question is raised, of course, only in respect of the higher forms of thinking, which involve the thinking of highly general or abstract objects and the judgment of similarities between them. And it is sometimes said that it is impossible to think of a general or abstract object, or, as is more commonly said, to form general and abstract ideas, without the aid of language. Now this can hardly be true; for in the mind of him who first discovers the similarity between classes of objects previously thought of separately, and who thus first thinks of the more general object, the apperceptive synthesis of systems must take place without the aid of a name for the more general object. By afterwards giving the object a name, he fixes it for his mind, and achieves a much greater power of thinking of it at will; and, further, he becomes able to communicate his new way of thinking to others, and to enable them also to think of the more general object. Names, then, are not essential to the thinking of general objects, but they greatly facilitate such thinking; they serve as ready means of bringing into play the mental systems corresponding to objects. In the case of general objects, they are much more serviceable for this purpose than the sense-impression made by any individual object of the class; for by such sense-impression one is led to think of the individual object with its specific peculiarities rather than of the general object : and when our aim is to discover truths about the class, the thinking of the features peculiar to individuals does but clog the processes of reasoning.   And the second great function of words is to fix and render communicable the results achieved by the thinking of successive generations of mankind. The language of any community thus embodies in objective form the intellectual progress made by it ; it reflects the mental structure of the individual minds, and enables and, indeed, compels each generation to build up its mental structure after the pattern set by foregoing generations.

Besides the two great processes by which there are developed in the mind dispositions and systems that enable it to think of a wealth of objects according to their intrinsic natures and affinities, there goes on a process of a different kind, as the result of which objects are thought of as related to form groups and series according to the accidents of time and place which have determined their conjunction for the mind. . That is to say, in addition to all that development of mental structure which partially mirrors the constitution of the world of objects, the mind's structure reflects also the history of the world in a very partial manner, namely, in so far as that history has been observed, whether directly

D

or indirectly, by the mind in question.
Objects are thought of together or in sequence,
because they are presented to the observation
of the subject as significant features of one
scene or of one train of incidents ; when the
mind has once perceived, or otherwise thought
of, particular objects as related parts of one
whole scene or train of events, it retains the
power (in some degree) of thinking of them
again in similar relations. This capacity to
think again of objects in the historical relations
in which they have been previously thought
of, implies the formation and persistence in
the mind of functional links between the
corresponding dispositions. The structure of
the developed mind comprises a vast system
of such links between its dispositions ; they
are generally spoken of as links of association,
and the objects are said to be associated
together for the mind. In virtue of the
existence of such links between dispositions,
the thought of any one object is apt to lead
the mind to think of another thus associated
with it. Thus, if I have on one occasion
seen a cat seated on the back of a pony, I
shall be apt to think of that cat whenever
I again think of that pony. The static
method describes the fact by saying that
the idea of the pony is associated with the
idea of the cat, and that the one idea, there-

fore, reproduces or tends to reproduce the other.

The formation of such associative links between dispositions is an important feature in the growth of the structure of the mind. It is obvious that the process is very different from the apperceptive processes of differentiation of dispositions and synthesis of systems which we have discussed above. Whereas these result in the capacity to think objects not previously thought, the associative process merely leads to the thinking of particular objects as standing to one another in some external relation, such as spatial proximity or temporal sequence.

The laws of such association and associative reproduction have been minutely studied, and much detailed knowledge of them has been acquired, which we cannot discuss here. The most important point to note is that the mind does not play a passive part in the formation of associations. Objects become associated for the mind, not merely because they are presented to the senses simultaneously or in immediate succession, but when and because the mind perceives or otherwise thinks of them as related with one another; and it does this only in so far as it is interested in them as so related, that is to say, in so far as they stir up some conative tendency. To go back to the instance of the pony and the cat ; if, at the moment my glance fell on the two animals, the cat had been seated on the ground at some little distance from the pony, I should have noticed both animals only in the most fleeting fashion, if at all, and I should not have associated them together. But their spatial relation implied a friendliness between them which is unusual and appeals to my interest in the behaviour of animals ; hence, out of all the details of the scene presented to my vision, my mind seizes upon these two objects and their relation. It may be remarked in passing that this example illustrates the impossibility of describing even so simple a process of association as this in terms of sensation and imagery. The mere spatial relation of the two visual forms is of no interest. It is only because they mean for me far more than is actually presented to the eye, that the situation appeals to an interest and draws my attention.

It is in virtue of the links of association thus formed between dispositions that we are able to reconstruct in memory the scenes and events we have lived through, an activity properly called reproductive imagination. In so far as this process is determined by the links between dispositions, one tends to re-think any series of events in the order in which they were first thought or perceived; the recounting of an incident by a person of simple mental type, who is merely talking for the sake of talking, reveals sometimes a mental process which is little more than the successive excitement of dispositions through associative links. But all such associative thinking is governed in some degree by the purpose or conation which maintains the activity; and this influence of the dominant purpose reveals itself in the selection and accentuation of the features or phases of the incident relevant to that purpose, and in the neglect and suppression of those which are irrelevant. The associative mechanism thus forms a quasi-mechanical part of the structure of the mind, and a part which functions in quasi-mechanical fashion; it furnishes material, as it were, for the creative activity of thought to work upon. In all consecutive thinking it plays some part, but its share in the determination of the course of mental activity varies widely. It plays a leading rôle in a simple faithful recital of events observed. In a recital dominated by æsthetic purpose, purposive selection and accentuation greatly modify its operation. In one in which the narrator, dominated by such a purpose, permits himself to embellish the story with additions as well as to select incidents, its rôle is still more subordinated

to creative activity. And in the composition
of a fictitious story, such as a novel or drama,
this dominance of associative reproduction
by purposive creative thinking is carried to
an extreme, though the activity still involves
the co-operation of the two processes. Such
composition, in so far as it is truly creative,
involves the apperceptive processes by which
mental dispositions and systems are developed ; in so far as it is reproductive, it
involves merely a selective preference among
the many alternative paths of association,
a preference determined by the purpose of the
artist.

We have distinguished two parts of the
mental structure directly concerned in cognition, namely, the part developed by apperceptive processes and consisting in the mental
dispositions and systems functionally related
in a manner that corresponds to the logical
relations between objects ; and, secondly, the
part developed by association and consisting
in associative links between dispositions and
systems, which links reflect the historical
sequence of events rather than any logical
relations. It seems worth while to illustrate
this distinction in the following way. Imagine
a pair of twins whose mental constitutions,
so far as inherited, are extremely alike.
Imagine them to be brought up in separate

places and in separate, though extremely similar, social circles, and to be subjected to closely similar educative processes. The result will be that in respect to " logical structure " their minds will be very similar, but in respect to " historical structure " very different. When set in similar situations, faced with similar problems or tasks, their mental processes would be very similar, and they would, as a rule, reach similar conclusions ; yet the particulars of their thinking would be constantly different ; they would be like two men thinking the same thoughts in different languages.

Hitherto we have considered the structure of the mind only in so far as it conditions cognition ; but we have seen that all thinking is affective and conative as well as cognitive. And knowing is but the servant of feeling and acting ; it is the process by which the will works towards its end and the satisfaction which comes with the attainment of the end ; and all the complex development of the conditions of the cognitive life, roughly indicated in the foregoing pages, is achieved through the efforts of the will to attain its ends.

Regarded from the biological point of view, the function of all mental process and mental structure is to preserve and promote the life of the race and that of the individual in so far as he subserves the life of the race. The life of the race is preserved and promoted by bodily activities ; of these the massive movements of the limbs and of other motor organs are of principal importance, and we may without serious error consider these alone. All mental activity, then, normally issues in bodily movement ; since only by promoting and guiding bodily movement can it fulfil its function. Conation is the application of mental energy to the direction and maintenance of the bodily activities by which the life of the race is furthered, and cognition governs bodily activity only through the medium of conation.

The primitive cycle of purposive or mental activity seems to be (as said above) cognition, evoking feeling and conation, which conation, issuing in bodily activity, brings about a new cognition that in turn brings a feeling of satisfaction and terminates the conation. For example, I become aware that the man standing beside me has struck me ; this cognition evokes in me angry feeling and an irresistible impulse to return the blow. The impulse immediately finds vent in action ; and I see the object of my thinking stretched out upon the ground. This new cognition terminates the conation, and my angry feeling gives place to satisfaction. Or it may be that the new cognition, the seeing of my fallen foe, evokes a feeling of pity and an impulse to succour him, which brings me to my knees beside him, and which only subsides and terminates in a feeling of satisfaction, when I see that he has suffered no serious hurt. In this case a second cycle of knowing, feeling, and striving, supervenes upon the first; and in this way the recurring cycle may be indefinitely prolonged.

The behaviour of animals and of young children frequently expresses such simple cycles of perceptual thinking. But the normal adult mind is so complexly organized that it seldom works in this simple fashion. In the situation suggested above, my cognition may be complicated by knowing that the man is drunk or otherwise irresponsible; or, in accordance with a general principle of conduct, I may restrain my angry impulse; or I may have learnt to replace the action in which the impulse naturally finds vent by some dexterous *jiu-jitsu* movement, which lays low my adversary even more effectually. Or the cycle of my activity initiated by the blow may be prolonged in the following way. My adversary dodges or effectually parries my blow; my thwarted impulse then waxes stronger, and I rush furiously upon him. A long struggle ensues, in which my angry impulse, repeatedly thwarted and repeatedly stimulated anew, brings into its service the whole energy of my organism; and my efforts are terminated only by the complete exhaustion of my available store of energy. This train of activity, which is almost wholly on the perceptual plane, consists in the repeated adaptation of my movements from moment to moment, as I perceive the new positions of my adversary; it is a recurring cycle of cognition, conation, and feeling, in which the conation, failing to attain satisfaction, persists and is but strengthened by each new cognition.

Or again, my angry impulse may be checked by one of fear, which prompts me to retreat. In this case, as soon as I am out of danger, I may think again of the incident; I live through it again in imagination, as we say. This restores the angry impulse; which, finding no satisfaction, in turn keeps me thinking of my adversary: the insult rankles in my bosom. Try how I may to turn my mind from this painful topic, I find myself repeatedly thinking of it; and, even when I succeed in thinking of other matters, my consciousness retains the disagreeable and angry tone. Quite involuntarily I find myself plotting out schemes of revenge; and perhaps, as I lie awake in the darkness of the night, I gnash my teeth and clench my fists and sweat and grow now hot now cold. The unsatisfied angry impulse drives me on to plan an elabor-

ate scheme of revenge. I imagine myself
meeting my adversary in a public place
and striking him a terrible blow. But then
I reflect that he is stronger than myself ; and
fear returns and checks and banishes this line
of thinking, which thus, even in imagination,
fails to bring me satisfaction. Then I think
of myself lying in wait for him on a dark night
and striking him down from behind with club
or gun ; or I concoct an elaborate plan by
which I can injure him in his business or his
social reputation.

Now, all this mental activity involved in
thinking out these schemes of action may be
not at all volitional in the proper sense of the
word. Volition begins when I attempt to
decide on executing one or other plan ; or
when I try to banish the whole matter from
my mind, or to pardon the offence. The
planning is a purposive activity ; but it may
be carried on wholly by the involuntary angry
impulse, which persists, because it has not
achieved its natural end, and because it keeps
bringing the incident back to my consciousness
and thus renewing itself by way of a vicious
circle. It may be asked—How can such a
train of purely mental activity as the planning
a line of action be said to conform to the
scheme we have laid down as typical, namely,
the cycle of cognition, conation, feeling, and

bodily activity, producing new cognition and again conation and feeling and bodily activity? For, it may be said, bodily activity is omitted from the cycle. The answer is, that the bodily activity in which each cycle of the thinking process issues, is only partially suppressed and disguised. We shall realize this, if we reflect on the behaviour in similar circumstances of a human being of a similar type, a savage or a child. The angry child, whose fear checks his impulse to immediate retaliation, runs off to a safe distance and then shouts out, " I'll get a big axe and chop off your head," perhaps suiting his actions to the words. That is his primitive planning of vengeance. Now, whether or no his words are accompanied by other bodily activity, their utterance is in itself a bodily activity ; the child is thinking or planning aloud ; and that is the natural and primitive way of thinking, in so far as one's thinking finds no other bodily expression : many savages and children commonly think aloud. The suppression of the actual utterance of the words used in the course of reflective thinking is a habit which we acquire under the influence of custom and of our natural tendency to economize energy ; but, though actual articulation may be suppressed, the use of words in the course of our thinking remains the equivalent of bodily activity ; the words play the same part ; in each cycle of the thinking, the conative impulse finds vent in a verbal formulation which initiates a new cycle.

We have now to face the problem of the way in which feeling and conation are determined by the structure of the mind. The question may at once be raised—Does each cognitive disposition determine not only knowing but also feeling and striving ? Is it at the same time affective and conative, as well as cognitive in function ? The answer to this question cannot be in doubt. The affective and conative organization of the mind is largely independent of and separate from its cognitive organization ; and there must exist, for the determination of these faculties, distinct dispositions which form an important part of the structure of the mind. Common speech and thought recognize this fact. For, as knowledge is the word used in popular speech to denote the structure of the mind in so far as it is cognitive, so the word character is used to denote its structure in so far as it is affective and conative. And we all recognize that the development of knowledge and of character are processes that by no means run strictly parallel, but are to a great extent independent of one another. We know also that our affective-conative attitude towards

an object may be radically transformed, while
our intellectual grasp of it remains practically
unchanged; as in the case, for example, of
some object, the thought of which at one
time evoked enthusiastic efforts on my part,
but which now leaves me cold or stirs in me
but a faint aversion and disgust. A common-
place and trifling example of such change
is the change of affective-conative attitude
towards a beefsteak which may be produced
in a hungry man by a full meal.

A much more difficult question is that of
the relation of the affective to the conative
organization of the mind. It is clear that, if
these are in any sense distinct organizations,
they are much more intimately bound up
together than they are connected with the
cognitive organization. We may, then, consider them as identical without risk of serious
error, and we shall not attempt to distinguish them or treat of them separately in
these pages.

The basis of character, or of the affective-
conative organization of the mind, seems to
consist in dispositions whose number, compared with that of the cognitive dispositions,
is small. Just as the latter may be regarded as
so many channels by which the cognitive faculties are directed upon corresponding objects;
so the conative dispositions may be regarded as

so many channels through which the conative faculty is directed to effect particular modes of bodily activity in relation to objects cognized. For, just as cognition is fundamentally a reaction of the mind of the subject upon impressions made by objects on its body (and only in the most highly developed minds attains relative independence of sense-impressions), so conation is fundamentally the direction of the mechanical processes of the body by the purposive activity of mind. And just as the various cognitive dispositions may in principle be regarded as having been differentiated from a single primitive disposition, so the conative dispositions of the developed mind may be regarded as having been differentiated from a single primitive disposition through which the conative faculty, the fundamental will to live, found expression.

This, of course, is a view of the evolutionary history of mind which, however plausible it may be, is a mere speculation. But we are on the sure ground of direct inference from facts of behaviour, when we describe the normal human mind as hereditarily endowed with a limited number of conative dispositions, each of which directs the conative energy to issue in a specific or characteristic mode of bodily activity. In the course of individual development each of these becomes

differentiated into a number of more highly
specialized dispositions, through the medium
of which conative energy issues in more
specialized modes of bodily activity. A single
illustration may suffice. Every normal woman
seems to be endowed with the maternal
impulse, which issues or tends to issue in
characteristic modes of bodily activity in
relation to her child ; this implies the possession of a corresponding conative disposition.
Among the women of each country, custom
determines that this disposition of relatively
low degree of specialization shall be differentiated to determine more highly specialized
bodily activities, which we call the expressions
of habits ; and each individual may further
specialize these habits in ways peculiar to herself. And through any such habit, or specialized differentiation of the maternal disposition
which is common to the race, the whole
energy of the maternal impulse may issue.

We have briefly indicated the nature of the
cognitive and of the conative structure of the
mind. It remains to describe equally briefly
the relations between these two sides. These
relations seem to be in the main of the nature
of associative links, a complex system of cross-
connexions between the dispositions of the
two kinds. In order to illustrate the formation of such cognitive-conative associations

and their influence upon the course of mental life, we may revert to the case (p. 104) of anger roused by an insulting blow and restricted in its expression by fear. Up to the time of the incident, I had been, we may suppose, as nearly as possible indifferent to my assailant; that is to say, his presence had evoked in me no well-defined feeling or attitude. But after the painful incident, I cannot think of him without fear, or anger, or both, and without desiring both to avoid him and to get the better of him in some way. Suppose, now, that circumstances repeatedly bring us together, and that his behaviour on such occasions is that of a bully covertly reminding me of the past insult that I dare not avenge. My attitude of blended anger and fear is renewed on each such occasion, and, being thus confirmed and rendered permanent, it becomes a full-blown sentiment of hatred. What development of the structure of my mind is implied by the growth of this sentiment? The emotion and impulse of anger and the specific bodily expressions and activities in which the impulse finds, or tends to find, vent, imply the possession of a complex conative disposition. The same is true of the emotional impulse of fear and its natural expression in bodily activity. On the other hand, my power of recognizing my assailant and of thinking of him in his absence implies the possession of a special cognitive disposition corresponding to that object. Further, the fact that, whereas I was formerly indifferent to this object, now I cannot think of him without anger or fear or a blending of the two emotions and attitudes, this fact, which we express by saying that I entertain a sentiment of hatred for him, implies that these two conative dispositions have become associatively linked with the cognitive disposition, and that these links have become permanent features of the structure of my mind.

The effect of such linkage is not only that, whenever the object of the sentiment is forced upon my attention, my thinking of him is coloured or suffused with these emotions, but also that I am rendered peculiarly apt to think of him. If I pass by a crowd of which he is a member, my eye singles him out and watches him furtively ; if we both have occasion to attend the same board-meeting, I am acutely aware of him and of all he says and does, though I may avoid glancing at him ; if I overhear his name mentioned by others in conversation, I am all agog to hear what is said. And this may continue in spite of my best efforts to cast out this demon of hatred and to resume my former attitude of indifference. Again, all my thinking of my adversary is biased by my attitude ; whatever I hear to his discredit I accept and retain, and I attribute his actions to the meanest motives ; until, by repetition of this process of selective thinking under the guidance of the specialized conative tendency, I come to think of him as a monster of iniquity.

Let us consider the influence on the cognitive life of the growth of a sentiment, in the light of a more agreeable instance. Imagine a light-hearted girl whose life has been a perpetual round of pleasures and social " duties." She marries and becomes a mother. The child upon her breast awakens in her the hitherto dormant maternal impulse, and all her delight is to watch and tend it, to describe its perfections and fondly to imagine its future in the brightest colours. Like the man harbouring the demon of hatred, she, too, seems possessed by a strong spirit ; but, if she could, she would not cast it out ; for it is the source of all her joy. Now, the maternal impulse with its accompanying tender emotion implies the existence of a corresponding conative disposition ; and the formation of the sentiment for the child involves the linking of this with the cognitive disposition which is the condition of all her thinking of the child ; and the new mode of life is the result of this linkage. Shortly after this change in her life she is left a widow ; now her affections are wholly given to her child, her whole being is devoted to it, and she tends it with passionate solicitude. The desire to secure its welfare becomes her dominant motive, to which all her thought and all her doing is subordinated. Perhaps she takes up the study of hygiene, masters the elements of physiology and the principles of clothing, of feeding, and of training in bodily habits ; if she is a very exceptional woman, she may even take up the study of psychology. All this intellectual activity and resultant expansion of her mental structure is prompted and sustained by the strong maternal impulse concentrated upon its one object. All her new knowledge is built up around her child, which she studies as assiduously as she tends it ; in virtue of its being the exclusive object of the strong sentiment of maternal love, the child becomes the nucleus about which a whole system of new knowledge, new interests, and new habits, is built up. The purposive energy which sustains and directs all these activities about the child and its welfare is that of the maternal impulse ; and the constant direction of this energy towards this particular object is the result of the development of the mental structure which is the sentiment of love for the child. For, though mother-love may seem to spring up almost full-blown, it is in reality a growth, subject to favourable and retarding influences; a system of tendencies which strengthens with use, atrophies with disuse, and only gradually attains its full strength and perfection. We realize this more clearly if we reflect upon other instances of maternal love; how, in a mother of several children, it may be concentrated wholly on one of them; how in a childless woman the maternal impulse may be evoked by some other object, a dog, or cat, or bird, and, becoming habitually directed to that object, may generate a sentiment strangely like maternal love.

Now, in order to bring home to our minds the full importance of such cognitive-conative linkage, let us carry the history of the devoted mother a step further. After some years of devotion, during which the sentiment has grown all-powerful and has generated a great system of knowledge, habits, and interests, the mother loses her child. She is prostrated with sorrow, and when the first paroxysm of grief is past, she remains inert; the mainspring of all her energy is stopped at its source; the will to live, which for years has poured itself freely through this one system, finds no adequate channel through which to animate her organism; and slowly she dies, her end probably hastened by the invasion of phthisis or of some other disease, which she no longer has the energy to resist. Or, if she continues to live, her best chance of restoration to a life of activity and health lies in the finding of some new object for her maternal impulse, to which the whole system of her master-sentiment may, with some readjustment, direct its activities, thus opening once more the choked channels by which alone the vital energy can adequately suffuse her whole being. She may turn to work on behalf of children in general, and find happiness in managing a children's hospital or in other good works; in which case the energy of the maternal impulse, being diverted or redirected, is said in technical language to be sublimated.

In the foregoing paragraphs we have illustrated the nature and growth of the functional connexions between cognitive and conative dispositions, taking strong and complex sentiments as our instances. The structure of the normal adult mind comprises many such sentiments of all degrees of strength and complexity, from what is called a passing fancy or aversion to strong, enduring, and highly complex sentiments of love and hate. In the structural basis of a complex sentiment a number of conative dispositions may be comprised. But the linkage of a conative disposition with any one cognitive system does not preclude it from becoming linked with others ; it may thus enter into the composition of sentiments for an indefinite number of diverse objects.   Thus each principal conative disposition must be regarded as linked with a considerable number of cognitive systems, by each of which it may be brought into activity, and through each of which in turn it pours its conative energy, thus maintaining its activities and promoting its further growth and differentiation.

It must be pointed out in passing that not only persons and places and material things may become the objects of sentiments, but also highly abstract and general objects, such as moral qualities, power, wealth, art.   Of some men it is no mere figure of speech to say that they love virtue or power or the Church, that they hate vice or dirt or disorder.   In respect of their growth and constitution, such sentiments seem to be subject to essentially the same principles as those directed to more concrete objects.   They constitute a most important part of the structure of the mind, since on them depends all that part of be-haviour which we call moral conduct.

CHAPTER IV

THE METHODS AND DEPARTMENTS OF PSYCHOLOGY

HITHERTO we have discussed only one of the methods of psychological study, namely, the indispensable preliminary description of consciousness or modes of thinking, by aid of introspection. Further, we have defined the central task of psychology as the description in general terms of the structure of the normal human mind, and of its modes of operation and development ; and we have indicated very roughly the kind of answers to these questions towards which the science seems to be working its way.

Now, there are many departments of psychology, distinguished either by the methods of inquiry pursued, or by the type or class of beings whose behaviour is studied by the psychologist. The former mode of division tends to assert itself in practice, because certain workers acquire special skill in the application of one or other method. But the division of the whole province of psychology on this principle is to be deprecated ; and the second principle is preferable.

Of the departments to be recognized as marked off according to the latter of these principles of division, the following are the chief :—

(1) The psychology of the normal human adult ; (2) the psychology of animals ; (3) the psychology of children ; (4) individual psychology, which attempts to define, and as far as possible to account for, the peculiarities of individual minds ; (5) the psychology of men in abnormal and diseased states of mind ; (6) social psychology, the study of the mass-mind and of its influence upon the individual mind in both its development and operation.

In each of these great departments all the available methods of study are applied. These methods fall under three principal heads :—(1) Introspection ; under this head is included not only the introspective observation of the psychologist, but also the study of the introspective statements or descriptions of other persons. This method is, of course, not available in the study of animals ; but in all the other departments it is applicable to various extents. (2) The observation and interpretation of behaviour, that is, of the purposive bodily activities in which the mental processes of men and animals find expression. (3) The study of the things created by mental and bodily activity, from the point of view of discovering what light they throw on the nature and operations of the minds which fashioned them ; thus, the nest of a bird, the web of a spider, a savage dance, a language, a code of laws or morals, a system of religious belief, a Gothic cathedral, a poem, a song, a child's drawing, the verses of a maniac, a game of skill or of chance, a trade-union, a system of government—all these, as well as every other product of human or animal activity, are capable of being studied from the psychological point of view, with more or less of profit.

It goes without saying that, wherever possible, these three great methods of study should be combined. Such combination is seldom possible, except in studying activities designedly induced under circumstances specially arranged and controlled. To study human or animal behaviour in this way is to make a psychological experiment. Much has been heard in late years of " experimental psychology," and it is often spoken of as though it were a distinct department of study. But that is by no means the case. Experiments may be, and are, made in every field of the province of psychology. Many persons find it difficult to imagine how experiment can be applied in psychological investigation ; the difficulty may be overcome by considering a few examples. I ask a friend to divide a straight line into two unequal parts in the way that seems to him to give the most pleasing or satisfying effect. The experiment may be made to combine the three great methods. I observe the behaviour of my subject as he takes his pencil and divides the line ; I measure the two parts into which he divides it ; and I ask him to describe as fully as possible how he came to choose just that point. Now, I can hardly hope to draw any valid and interesting conclusion from a single experiment of this sort. But suppose that I repeat it with fifty persons, and that I find a striking uniformity in the products of their activity, namely, that the great majority divide the line in such a way that the length of the shorter is to that of the longer part very nearly as $1 : 1.6$. Knowing that, if the shorter is to the longer as $1 : 1.618$, then the longer bears the same ratio to the sum of the two lengths, and noticing that the average of all the proportions chosen by the fifty subjects approximates very closely to this ratio, I repeat the experiment with more subjects. Suppose, then, I find that the larger the number of subjects whose results are averaged, the closer this approximation becomes. Here, surely, would be an indication of an experimentally established law of human behaviour of considerable interest, well fitted to stimulate any alert mind to seek for an explanation. The result would make it seem worth while to study closely both the behaviour and the introspective reports of the subjects, as well as the products of their activity. It may be added that an indication of this law may be obtained by the application of the third method alone, namely, by studying the proportion of objects in common use and of the parts of decorative designs. But it is obvious that, for the accurate establishment and investigation of this general tendency, experiment affords indispensable aid.

As another example of experiment we may take the following:—I try to write down continuously a familiar verse, while I repeat aloud other equally familiar verses, and I ask other persons to attempt the same task. Here again all three methods of study are applicable and instructive, namely, introspection, the observation of behaviour, and the study of the product; observations of these three kinds supplement one another and throw considerable light on the question of the possibility of thinking of two things at once.

But the most profitable experiments are generally those which are designed to provide an answer to some definite question. For example, it may be asked—In learning a passage of prose or verse by heart, can I learn it with fewest repetitions by reading it again and again without intermission ? Or shall I do better by allowing an interval to elapse after each reading ; or by grouping my readings in short series separated by intervals of time ? And, if the second or third distribution of the readings is most advantageous, what interval is most favourable ? For clearly there must be such a most favourable interval.

It has been found that questions such as these can readily be answered by a little careful experimenting, and that the answers to many such questions can be stated as empirical rules which hold good within definable limits for all normal subjects. The possibilities of applying experiment, illustrated by the few simple examples mentioned above, have been actively exploited during the last half-century ; many ingenious methods of experiment and many useful pieces of apparatus have been devised ; and, since the conduct of experiments which involve the use of apparatus of any complexity demands a properly fitted laboratory, there has grown up within the field of experimental psychology a more special field of laboratory psychology. But, though owing to practical necessities there is a tendency to regard this as a separate department, like experiment in general it consists merely in special refinements of the three great methods of observation which are applicable in the various departments. Experimental observation and laboratory methods are most extensively applied in the first of the departments of our list (p. 121), namely, the psychology of normal human adults : for only with well-trained adult subjects can the most complete experiments be made ; only in such subjects can we hope to find the necessary patience and scientific conscience ; and only from them can we hope to obtain uniformly trustworthy introspective reports. Nevertheless, experiments, and even the laboratory methods of experiment, are now largely used in other departments, especially in the study of children and of patients suffering from mental disorders. In the field of child-study they are being applied with especial vigour and enthusiasm to the elucidation of many educational problems ; such problems as the following :—What are the most effective methods of learning by heart ? What is the effect upon memory in general of practice in committing to heart verses or other matter ? To what extent, if any, does the study of algebra improve the pupil's ability to master arithmetic or geometry ? Are there any advantages in appealing to two or more senses whenever possible, instead of to eye or to ear alone ? In what way and in what degree can the power of visual imagination be profitably developed by special exercises? In what way does the fatigue induced by the wage-earning of "half-timers" and evening scholars affect their school work? These are a few out of hundreds of questions, answers to which (of the first importance for educational practice and policy) can only be obtained by systematic experimenting.

Even in the study of animals, where we cannot hope for introspective reports to help us in the interpretation of the behaviour we observe, experiment is now much used. If, for example, we throw to a chicken a grub or caterpillar of nauseous flavour, and observe its behaviour towards this kind of grub on the first and subsequent occasions, we repeat an experiment which has become famous and found its way into scores of books on psychology. Or we may confine a white rat in a cage, the only outlet from which is a passage with several turns and blind alleys opening from it; by observing its behaviour in escaping on successive occasions, we may get some notion of its capacity to "learn the way out"; and, by modifying the conditions, we can learn on which senses the animal chiefly relies in the process of learning. Or we may allow a monkey to learn to extract nuts from a box by manipulating a simple piece of mechanism; and then, by putting his nuts in a differently constructed box, we may discover how far he is aided by his familiarity with the former mechanism in the task of solving the similar but rather different problem. Such observation under natural and experimental conditions of the behaviour of animals of all grades, from the microscopic amoeba to the dog and the still more highly intelligent chimpanzee, or the mysteriously co-operating ants and bees, is now one of the most actively pursued departments of psychology ; it offers an inexhaustible field for inquiry, which becomes ever more fascinating and profitable the further our knowledge advances.

It has been said that measurement is the essence of science, that where there can be no measurement there can be no science. From this premise it has sometimes been argued that there can be no science of psychology ; for, it was said, states of consciousness are incapable of being measured. The conclusion cannot be accepted. The argument is simply a mass of error and confusion. Without delaying to expose it in detail, it may be pointed out that the premise is a wholly unwarranted piece of dogmatism. Several of the generally recognized sciences owe little or nothing to measurement, and they would lose but little of their scientific character if all exact measurement were banned from them ; such, for example, are geology and most of the biological sciences. Further, measurement, and even exact measurement, is possible in psychology, and has been extensively applied. We can measure the accuracy of judgments of many kinds, *e.g.* of judgments of weight by the hand, of pitch by the ear, of brightness, of colour-tone, or of length, by the eye ; in such cases, by aid of simple apparatus and rules of procedure, we can measure with any desired degree of refinement the average error of judgment of a given subject under constant conditions ; and we can express the accuracy of his power of judging in terms of this average error ; or we can detect the influence of certain disturbing conditions which tend to induce erroneous judgment, and accurately measure the magnitude of that influence. It follows that we can measure the influence of a variety of conditions upon the accuracy of judgments of many kinds ; for example, the influence of practice and of fatigue, of prepossession or bias. We can measure also the duration of many mental processes to within a few thousandths of a second. And we can measure the rate of execution and repetition and the accuracy of performance of many mental tasks.

A kind of measurement of especial value and wide application in psychology is the counting the number of repetitions of a process

E

involved in the execution of a given task : for example, the number of repetitions required to commit a given quantity of verbal matter to memory, or to re-learn it to the same degree of perfection after a given interval; the number of repetitions of a particular combination of movements required in order to render it automatic or independent of attentive control ; the number of momentary glances at a picture or at such an object as a series of printed numbers, letters, or words, that the subject must take in order to apprehend every detail.

In all these and in other ways, data are being accumulated from which conclusions of many kinds can be drawn ; and, since for many purposes large masses of such numerical data secured by experiment are required as the basis for general conclusions, the opportunity arises of submitting the figures to mathematical treatment and of extracting from them in this way much knowledge which otherwise would remain hidden. There is thus growing up what is sometimes regarded as a special department, namely, mathematical psychology, but which is a special development of experimental method applicable in the several departments, rather than itself a department.

A few words must be said of another line

of study which makes some claim to be regarded as a special department under the title physiological psychology. We only know mind or purposive activity as embodied in organisms ; and, since our cognitive processes are largely determined by physical impressions made on our sense-organs and transmitted from them along the nerves to the brain, and since our conative processes guide and control bodily activities through the medium of the brain and nerves, it follows that the psychologist cannot be indifferent to all the knowledge of the organs of the body gained by the detailed study of them by the methods of physiology. Therefore, in each department, the student of behaviour must master as fully as possible all that the anatomists and physiologists can tell him of the structure and functions of the organs, especially of the nervous system and sense-organs, of the living beings he studies. It would, for example, be absurd to discuss the mental powers of insects in ignorance of the peculiar structure of their eyes, or to attempt to account for the peculiar mental state of the aphasic patient without any knowledge of the nature and effects of brain injuries of the kind to which his sudden loss of the power of speech is due. For the bodily organs and their processes are the media through which the mind is kept in touch both with the world of material objects and with other minds ; and the purposive control and guidance of these processes is from the biological standpoint the prime and immediate function of mind. Physiological psychology is, then, not a province or department, but rather a method applicable within each department, a method which supplements at many points the three great methods of psychological observation. It may also be regarded as a debatable ground in which physiology, with its mechanical explanations, and psychology, with its explanations in terms of purpose, come together, affording each other what help they can, yet each striving to extend its principles of explanation as widely as possible, in order to make good its claim to explain the facts of behaviour, and to absorb its rival by making of it a department of itself.

We sometimes hear also the expression "comparative psychology" used in a way that implies the existence of a special department of that name. But this usage, again, is misleading ; there is no such department ; rather every department is, or should be, comparative, in so far as it does, or could, use the comparative method ; that is to say, in so far as in attacking its special problems, it does, or could, bring the observations and conclusions or other departments to its aid.

These general remarks upon the methods and departments of psychology may be concluded by pointing out that each department has, as it were, a double life and purpose. On the one hand it contributes what it can towards the solution of what we have called the central problems of psychology, the problems of the structure, functioning, and genesis of the normal human mind. On the other hand it has problems and a field of applications peculiar to itself, in relation to which it devises special methods of study, produces a highly specialized literature, and is prosecuted by bands of specialized workers, who too often, it must be admitted, show themselves indifferent to, or ignorant of, the problems, methods and results of other departments.

In the following pages it remains to consider how each of the departments of psychology is meeting its special problems, and how each is contributing to forward the central work of the science, the discovery of the laws of function, structure, and genesis of the normal human mind.

The first department on our list, the study of the normal human adult, which, until the modern period, was the only branch of psychology seriously pursued, must always hold its place as in some sense the most important ;

for its work is to deliver the frontal attack upon the central fortress. Nevertheless, it is now evident that the frontal attack cannot hope to succeed without the aid of the other lines of advance. Sixty years ago this department, which then was the whole of the science, was thought, even by some of its exponents, to have wellnigh achieved its task; but now we can see that it had not gained sight of the greater part of the difficulties before it, and that it had done nothing more than survey the outermost walls and capture a few of the advanced posts of the fortress. For in this science, more than in any other, a most difficult task is the first and indispensable one of discovering and formulating the problems to be solved. This appearance of finality was due merely to the fact that the old method of unaided introspection was incapable of advancing our knowledge beyond the point to which it had already carried it.

The main work of this department falls under two heads: first, to carry to an ever greater pitch of refinement the introspective description of mental process by the aid of the new experimental methods; secondly, to bring to bear upon the central problems all the new light provided by the work of the other departments. Of the nature of the experimental work some slight indications

have been given in the preceding chapter.
It is too highly technical for further description in these pages. The new light provided
by the other departments and its bearing on
the central problems can be best discussed in
briefly reviewing each of these departments in
turn.

CHAPTER V

THE STUDY OF ANIMAL BEHAVIOUR

LONG ago the great Greek thinker, Aristotle,
initiated the study of animal behaviour and
set it in its true relation to the psychology
of man. He taught that the behaviour of
animals is the expression of powers of purposive control which are exercised by man
also ; the difference between man and animals
being the possession by man of powers which
the animals do not possess, in addition to
those which they have in common with him.
But, after this good beginning, more than
two thousand years elapsed before the study
was taken up again from this sound standpoint.
At the dawn of the era of modern science,
Descartes, perhaps the most influential philo-
sopher of the seventeenth century, 'put off
the time of this return to the true line of progress by contending that, while men's actions

are governed by the will and purpose of a
reasoning soul, animals are merely complex
machines—that all their movements are fully
explicable by the mechanical principles which
enable us to construct, control, and understand the movements of a clock, or a pump,
or any other piece of mechanism.

Hardly less prejudicial to the study of
animal behaviour was the doctrine of instinct,
which was for a long time the only rival
of Descartes' theory. It was a theological
rather than a scientific doctrine. In so far
as it was in any sense scientific, it was of the
old " faculty psychology " ; and it affords the
clearest example of the pernicious effects
exerted by the misuse of the notion of faculties.
The actions of men were said to be governed
by the faculty of reason, those of animals
by the faculty of instinct ; and this attribution
of the actions of animals to instinct seems to
have disguised from most of those who used
the word the need for further study or explanation of them. It was a striking example
of the power of a word to cloak our ignorance
and to hide it even from ourselves. Those
who tried to go behind the word, to seek some
further explanation of animal behaviour,
usually represented the instinctive acts of
animals as directly guided by the hand of
God. Now it would be presumptuous to

assert that they are not guided by the hand of God ; but, however firmly we may believe that the world, and especially the world of life, is in some sense the working out of the design of a beneficent Creator, we have to recognize that men cannot escape responsibility for the intelligent direction of their own lives and those of their humbler fellow-creatures. This responsibility implies the obligation to obtain wherever possible the kind of understanding, both of our own natures and of those of animals, that will enable us to control as fully as possible the course of events.

Early in the nineteenth century, the great French naturalist, Lamarck, began the work of setting the study of animal behaviour on its modern lines by propounding his theory of animal evolution ; according to this theory, new forms arise by the transmission to off-spring of the adaptations of structure and function achieved by the parent. But it was not until the work of Charles Darwin, especially his theory of natural selection, convinced the world that all the forms of life, man not excepted, had been continuously evolved from some simple primordial form, that the problem of the relation of the human to the animal mind excited a widespread interest and began to be seriously studied. Darwin himself had argued that, just as the human body with all its wonderful perfections of structure and function seems to have been evolved by a long series of minute steps from the body of some animal species allied to the existing manlike apes, so also all the structure and functions of his mind must be regarded as having been evolved by a similar series of minute steps from the mind of the same animal ancestor. (See Geddes & Thomson : *Evolution.*)

Herbert Spencer also had propounded independently of Darwin a theory of continuous evolution which implied the evolution of the mental powers of man from those of animals ; he had attempted to show how the brain of man may be supposed to have been gradually evolved by steps of increasing complexity of organization from a nervous system of very simple type, such as is found in some lowly animals ; and he had assumed that the evolution of the powers of the mind had run parallel with that of the nervous system, and that each step of mental evolution might in fact be regarded as the effect or expression of a corresponding step of nervous evolution.

These views naturally excited violent opposition in many quarters ; for they were felt to endanger the privileged position which man had assumed to be his, and to be inconsistent in many ways with the generally accepted doctrines of religion. The old antagonism between religion and science was fanned into a new flame, and there was waged a violent controversy, the faint rumblings of which may still be heard by an attentive ear.

These new doctrines and the consequent controversies gave a great stimulus to the study of animal behaviour ; and much accurate knowledge has been accumulated by these studies. But it cannot be said that the principal questions in dispute have been finally settled. The continuity of mental evolution of man from lower forms has in the main been accepted, though a few authoritative voices still protest against this acceptance. It is generally admitted that we may confidently accept the doctrine of continuity of mental evolution throughout the animal world ; but it is pointed out that, between the mind of man and that of the highest animal there is an enormous gap ; and it is urged that we cannot legitimately suppose this great gap to have been bridged by the slow processes of evolution. It is further urged that there are differences of kind as well as of degree between the powers of the human and those of the animal mind. To the first of these objections the thoroughgoing evolutionist returns two overwhelming replies. It is admitted, he says, that the degrees of development of mental

powers in the animal kingdom run parallel
in the main with the degrees of development
of the nervous system. Now, between the
nervous system of man and that of the highest
animal there is in the scale of complexity of
organization an enormous gap, which corresponds to the gap in the scale of mental powers ;
and we have, therefore, good reason to believe
that, if we could observe the animals whose
nervous systems filled the gap in the scale of
nervous organization, we should find that
they possessed mental powers which filled the
corresponding gap in the scale of mental
organization. The second reply of the evolutionist supplements the first in a very effective
manner, as follows. The study of the bodily
and mental development of human beings
shows that each one of us, in the course of
his growth from a microscopic germ in his
mother's womb to adult life, exhibits, as regards both his bodily and his mental powers
and organization, a continuous evolution :
at no point does any new factor suddenly
appear ; but, in accordance with the well-
established law of recapitulation, both the
organization of the nervous system and the
development of mental capacity progress continuously, roughly reproducing in their successive stages similar stages of the course of
racial evolution. If, then, the child can cross

in the course of some few years the great gap
in the scale of mental organization, how can
we with any plausibility deny that the race
may have crossed the same gap in the course
of millions of years ?

As regards the contention that the powers of
the human mind differ not only in degree, but
also in kind, from those of the animals ; it is
to be noted that it raises a difficulty for the
doctrine of the continuity of mental evolution,
only if it is accepted as meaning that the
human mind has powers of which no feeblest
germ or trace is indicated by the behaviour
of animals. Now, it is generally recognized
that Darwin, and many of his immediate
followers, biased, perhaps, to some extent
by the desire to diminish the gap between
the human and the animal mind, seriously
over-estimated the mental powers of the higher
animals, putting upon their behaviour in
many cases anthropomorphic interpretations
which were not justifiable. Nevertheless,
though we severely restrain this tendency to
exalt the mental powers of animals above their
true level, the gap no longer seems so wide as
it did half a century ago ; for the new insight
into the nature of mental processes brought
by the study of animals has diminished the
gap from the human side, by showing us
that in important respects human mental

processes are more like those of the animals than had previously been supposed.

Philosophers had agreed with popular tradition in describing man as a rational being and attributing all his actions and beliefs to reasoned motives and logical operations. For, studying chiefly or solely their own minds, which no doubt approximated more nearly than any others to the ideal of a purely rational mind, they overlooked the fact that much of human behaviour is the outcome of crude impulses and desires which reason cannot approve and the will cannot control; and they overlooked also the fact that a large proportion of the beliefs which are expressed in the conduct of the average man have been acquired by processes of an alogical nature and are incapable of being justified by logic.

When we have made such necessary corrections in our estimates of the minds of men and animals, we have to admit, indeed, that the gap between them is immense; but we may agree with the preponderant opinion among competent persons, which asserts that the mental functions of man present no such radical difference in kind as would forbid us to believe in the continuity of mental evolution; for evidence of some rudiment of every type of mental function may be discovered in animal behaviour.

The study of animal behaviour has hitherto taught us three lessons of high importance for psychology : (1) it has made clearer the nature of mental or purposive activity, and has revealed its prevalence throughout the whole of the animal world ; (2) it has elucidated the very bases of human nature by displaying in relative simplicity among the animals the modes of activity which constitute that basis, but which in human life are so complicated and obscured by the great development of our intellectual nature that they for long eluded almost completely the penetration of philosophers ; (3) it has shown us how we have to conceive in its main outlines the course of evolution which has culminated in the human mind.   We may devote a few words to each of these topics.

The kind of purposive activity with which each of us is most familiar is the voluntary striving to bring about some state of affairs which he has clearly conceived beforehand, which he has judged to be desirable or good, and which he has deliberately designed and resolved to bring about.   Of such an activity he can say—I act thus and thus in order to achieve this end, which I desire to see achieved because, contemplating it in idea, I foresee that its realization will bring me satisfaction. Such activity, therefore, becomes for us the type of purposive activity ; and, when we are able to infer that the activity of any other being conforms to the same type, we feel that we understand it or can explain it. But there remains a deeper question : Why should the attainment of the particular end afford me satisfaction ? The answer to this question that was most commonly accepted, before the study of animal behaviour had made some progress, ran as follows : Because I have found on former occasions that a situation, similar to that which I desire to bring about, gives me pleasure or eases me of pain. Such increase of pleasure or diminution of pain was thus regarded as the goal of all purpose and volition, the object of all the desires that are the motives of our actions. It was admitted that a far-sighted man might prefer distant pleasures of great magnitude to the lesser pleasures of present bodily ease, and that he might even choose to suffer pain, if it seemed a necessary step to the attainment of the greater pleasures : and thus was explained such facts as that Christian martyrs without number had chosen to suffer at the stake and in the arena rather than to renounce their faith ; for, it was said, they believed that by so doing they would secure the very intense and lasting pleasures of heaven and escape the enduring tortures of hell.

This theory of human motives (known as psychological hedonism) was made the basis of a philosophy of morals and politics which claimed to be complete and ultimate, and which has exercised a great and beneficent influence throughout the civilized world and has done much to shape our laws and institutions; namely, the Utilitarian philosophy. But the study of animal behaviour has led us to see that this theory of motives was false. When the behaviour of animals was studied without prejudice, it became apparent that the animal world also has its martyrs. Many an animal-mother strives with all the energy of her being against overwhelming odds and, un-flinching, meets death in its most cruel form, rather than desert her young to seek an easy safety in flight. Yet, what nice calculation of the balance of pleasure over pain can be supposed to sustain her efforts? She surely has no unshakable belief in heavenly rewards or hellish punishments! Nor can we suppose that she dreads the pain of remorse that may follow upon her desertion of her post. She takes no thought of the morrow, anticipates neither good nor evil, neither pleasure nor pain; but, heedless of all consequences, she makes one supreme self-sacrificing effort to fulfil the purpose of her being, to hand on the torch of life undimmed. In her frail organism runs one slender stream of the great purpose which animates all living beings, whose end we can only dimly conceive and vaguely describe as the perpetuation and increase of life.

Such instances of animal self-sacrifice are well suited to arrest our attention and to set us thinking, and indications of the truth to which they so clearly point may be seen on every hand in the world of animal behaviour. This simple but profound truth is that in particular situations animals behave in this or that way, striving persistently, often putting forth all their energy to the point of exhaustion, because in each case it is the creature's nature so to do, under the given conditions. The solitary wasp laboriously drags to her carefully prepared nest the prey secured by a day's hunting, and seals it there together with her egg, in order that it may serve as food for the offspring which she will never see, and of whose needs or existence she can have no knowledge. The young bird flies a thousand miles across land and sea, seeking, she knows not why, the climate best suited to her young. She builds her nest according to the pattern of the species and broods over her eggs ; experiencing, we may suppose, a continued satisfaction in the progress of her work ; but without, we may confidently say, once thinking of the young birds to whose welfare all her labours are directed. The young male nightingale, arriving in the spring from his distant winter haunts, takes up his station in a dense bush and pours forth night after night and all day long his flood of music, without any conscious anticipation of the mate whom his song will bring to his side ; though, when she comes, he knows well how to welcome her. The young horse snorts and shies at the dark object crouched upon the roadside, though it is thousands of years since the wolves laid in wait for his ancestors. The town-bred, domesticated, well-fed terrier cannot resist the smell of the rabbit on the grass, and follows the trail in wild excitement, deaf to his master's call ; though he knows nothing of ground game and has never before set eyes or nose on a rabbit.

In all these and in countless other instances of animal behaviour we see the same fact— the animal is impelled to act as he does, at each step foreseeing at most the immediate consequence of his acts and nothing of the remote ends subserved by them. Must we, then, go back to the doctrine of Descartes, and conclude that what we call the purposive activities of animals are in reality purely mechanical processes, differing only in complexity from those of any man-made machine,

and that the actions of man alone of all
living beings are directed and sustained by
purpose ?

This we must refuse to do for two good
reasons. First, the actions of the animals,
from the simplest to the highest, present
those outward or objective marks of purpose
on which we have throughout insisted ;
namely, persistent direction towards their
proper ends in spite of all obstacles and difficulties, with variation in detail of the modes of
activity. Secondly, if we look with unbiased
eyes at the human comedy, refusing to be
blinded by a stupid pride and the traditional
contempt for our humbler fellow-creatures, we
shall see that much of our behaviour is strictly
analogous to these characteristic actions of
the animals. When the young infant first
cries aloud his discomfort, he has no knowledge
of the hands or of the breast that will succour
him. When at the first crack of thunder the
child (or the adult) runs trembling to hide
himself in the nearest dark corner, he has no
conception of any hurtful power that he will
elude in his hiding-place. When the modest
maiden puts the last touches to her toilet,
blushing at her own loveliness, she would find
it difficult to account for her behaviour in
terms of purpose. When Romeo's admiring
gaze follows her and sends her fleeing in a

strange confusion, or when she lingers a
moment and casts one backward glance, she
may in perfect truthfulness deny all knowledge of the natural end of her activities.
And, even when later she submits to his
embrace, she may do so without any anticipation of pleasure or of pain and without
foreseeing one step of the way on which her
foot is set. She is merely fulfilling the purpose of her being, prompted to each action
as the circumstances arise by impulses but
little, if at all, less blind than those of the
nesting bird.

Romeo, too, when bright eyes spur him on
to redoubled efforts in the game of strength
and skill or lend a new music to his voice,
may know as little as the nightingale pouring
out his song what end is subserved by his
reckless output of energy.

Or consider this strong man in the prime
of life, impelled by ambition to strain all the
powers of his cultivated intellect in the
pursuit of worldly success. His course of
life may be carefully planned out for many
years to come and steadily pursued. He is
the very type of strong purpose and resolution ;
but ask him : Why does he pursue this
ambition, why strive so persistently after a
high place ? And you may find that he
cannot tell you. He well knows that worldly

success is dust and ashes ; that fame is only
valued so long as we have it not ; that he could
easily obtain a wealth of pleasures which he
now forgoes. All he can tell you is—He is
built like that. By choosing a long series
of types of human and animal activity, we
might construct a scale which, by minute
steps of difference, would lead down from the
most truly purposive actions of man, actions
sustained and renewed through long years by
a firm self-conscious resolution to achieve
some clearly conceived end, to the actions of
the simplest microscopic animalcule. Rather
than separate the animals from man and
assign them to the realm of mechanism, or
than fly at once to the extravagant conclusion
that our conviction of the purposive nature
of our highest activities is a mere delusion
and that man also is but a piece of complex
machinery ; rather than consent to put aside
our problem with this unjustifiable and, in
any case, wholly premature conclusion, we
must revise and widen our notion of purposive activity. Instead of taking the most
developed modes of human volition as the
type and form of all purposive activity, we
must recognize that these higher modes, in
which some remote end of the activity is
clearly conceived and willed, are but the most
rare and highly specialized varieties of a great

genus which includes all modes of human and animal behaviour.

The truth is that volition springs out of blind impulse, presupposes it, and is only a higher development of it, brought about by a higher organization of the structure of the mind in both its cognitive and conative aspects. When the ambitious man forms and pursues his resolution to achieve a high place among his fellows, he does so only in virtue of the fact that the structure of his mind comprises a conative disposition the excitement of which impels him, or gives rise to an impulse which drives him on, to assert himself, to display himself, before his fellow-men. Only in virtue of his possession of this specifically directed disposition does a great position appear to him a desirable object ; if it were lacking in his constitution, the desires of other men for such a position would seem to him inexplicable and absurd. Only in virtue of the possession of a specialized conative disposition, does the innocent youth find his glances, his steps, his thoughts, irresistibly turning to the maiden ; only in virtue of this, is he filled with a vague unrest and a longing for he knows not what, a longing which makes all other ends and pursuits seem trivial and unreal ; only in virtue of this, is he liable to be seized with what others, who have partially forgotten or never experienced it, speak of as the strange madness of romantic love.

Thus, just as truly as the actions of the animals, all instances of human activity (even the most truly volitional and self-consciously directed) imply the operation of special dispositions through which the conative energy, the will to live, is directed to prompt and sustain particular modes of action ; each of these conative dispositions may generate either a mere blind impulse, or a desire for an end more or less clearly conceived. The great differences between the simpler and the higher modes of activity are of two kinds : first, the differences in the degree of clearness and fulness with which the natural end, which alone can satisfy the impulse in each case, is thought of and the steps towards its attainment planned out ; secondly, the differences in the degree to which the one impulse co-operates or conflicts with other impulses in more or less complex fashion, according to the complexity of organization of the mind's structure.

The second great lesson, learnt in the main through the study of animal behaviour, is that each human mind does not, as so many of the older writers assumed, start upon its career like a blank sheet of paper or a smooth tablet of wax, equally ready to receive and retain whatever impressions the outer world may make upon it, and endowed merely with the power of re-shuffling and reproducing in fainter forms these vivid sensory impressions. Or, to put the matter in another way, it has taught us that each individual organism, human or animal, begins its active career either with some considerable part of its full mental structure, both cognitive and conative, already perfected, or, if with but little perfected structure, still with much in the way of innate tendencies to the development of structure.

The necessity of believing in the transmission from generation to generation of such innate tendencies to the development of mental structure is most obviously forced upon us by the behaviour of some of the insects; for in the insect world the innately determined structure of the mind is commonly very complex, and constitutes a larger proportion of the total structure than in any other of the higher branches of the tree of life. Of all the insects, the solitary wasps, perhaps, illustrate our present thesis in the most striking manner. There are many species which prey upon insects and other small creatures; these creatures are generally killed or paralysed by stinging, and then are packed away and sealed up in a nest or burrow together with one or more eggs of the wasp,

there to serve as food to the grub which
after a time will emerge from the egg. Now
the features of this process, of especial interest
from our present point of view, are two :—
First, the wasps of each species (with few
exceptions) prey on animals of one kind only,
although in all probability the grubs of each
species might flourish on animal food of almost
any kind ; one species of wasp preys on cater-
pillars only, another on grasshoppers, a third
on spiders, and so on ; and a wasp may spend
many hours searching for her proper prey
amidst an abundance of other small creatures
which seem equally well adapted to serve as
food for her grubs. This choice of her proper
prey is not the result of imitation of other
wasps of the same species, nor of any other
process of learning ; for the wasp hatches out
from the isolated chrysalis as a fully adult
insect, and shortly proceeds to seek her prey.
The wasp, then, has innate power of recognizing her proper prey, or, in the sense in
which we have defined the word knowledge,
she must be said to have innate knowledge
of her prey ; that is to say, she inherits a
cognitive disposition which renders her capable
of knowing her prey, when it comes within
range of her sense-organs. The second point
of interest in the present connexion is that
the wasp of each species handles her prey in

a manner peculiar to her species ; one always
stings her caterpillar in a peculiarly effective
manner : another walks backwards as she
drags her prey to her nest ; this mode of
progression gives her more power in dragging
large specimens of the kind she preys upon,
but she behaves in the same way when the
specimen is so small that she could easily
run forward with it raised in her jaws ; it is
as though a man should stagger home with
bent back and bowed legs, under the weight
of a pound of tea slung on his shoulders : a
third always straddles across the body of
her victim as she carries it off : one species
always holds her prey with her third pair of
legs, another with the second pair ; others
hold it in the jaws. And, when the wasp
arrives at her nest with her prey, her behaviour
again runs on stereotyped lines ; one species
invariably lays down her prey and runs into
the hole she has prepared, turns about, and
drags in her prey after her ; another suspends
it on the crotch of some low branching plant,
while she explores her nest ; a third carries
hers directly into the nest without preliminary exploration. This constancy of mode
of behaviour of each species in the normal
course of their activities might seem at first
sight to favour the view of those who regard
animals as mere machines (and that such

insects as wasps are unconscious mechanisms has been seriously maintained by some modern observers) ; yet these same wasps are capable of intelligently adapting their behaviour to unusual circumstances, and they display in certain respects very striking idiosyncrasies.

Such exhibition of complex modes of nicely adapted behaviour without previous experience of the situation, and the constancy of such modes throughout a species, are the two most generally accepted marks of instinctive action. For the word "instinctive" survives as a general descriptive term for activities of this kind ; though modern science is no longer content to use it as a cloak for ignorance, and to regard such actions as explained by attributing them to a faculty of instinct : it uses the word rather to mark the need for a theory. The foregoing examples of instinctive behaviour, considered in connexion with the general account of mental structure given on earlier pages, indicate clearly what our theory of instinct must be. The recognition of her specific prey by the wasp of each species, without any guidance from her previous experience, implies the possession of a corresponding cognitive disposition, which is provided in the innate constitution and becomes functionally perfect in each individual without being exercised. The handling of her prey by each individual in the manner characteristic of her species on her first encounter with it, similarly implies the possession of a corresponding innate conative disposition. And the fact that each wasp reacts in this specific fashion to her specific prey, and to that alone, implies that this conative disposition is innately linked with the cognitive disposition that enables her to recognize her prey. This, then, is the nature of an instinct, the mental structure which is the condition of an instinctive action : it consists in a more or less highly specialized conative disposition linked with a specialized cognitive disposition ; the whole cognitive-conative system being innate or inherited, that is to say, developing spontaneously in each individual to a state in which it is capable of determining appropriate reaction to its object.

This is the formula by which we may in a sense explain a large part of the behaviour of all animals ; namely, all those purposive reactions which imply perceptual discrimination of the object without previous experience of it. Wellnigh the whole of the behaviour of some animals conforms strictly to this type. The best examples of lives governed wholly by instinct are provided by some of the insects, which, emerging from the chrysalis with all their organs and capacities fully developed, straightway perform a single cycle of highly complex purposive actions, and die. The structure of the mind of such an animal must be conceived as consisting of a limited number of innate cognitive dispositions, each linked with a conative disposition; and the maintenance of the single cycle of activities, which compose the life history of the adult creature, depends on the fact that the exercise of each conative disposition produces a situation which excites another cognitive disposition, which in turn sets to work another conative disposition, and so on, until the cycle is completed. Such, for example, is the behaviour of an insect which, after hatching out, flies about until it encounters a certain flower, settles upon it, and, by a series of precise manipulations of its parts, deposits its eggs among the ovules of the flower, that is, in the one situation in all the world in which the eggs can develop.

But most of the animals perform their instinctive actions more than once in the course of their lives; and, when any such action is repeated many times, we can generally observe that the nature of the activity becomes modified in accordance with experience, modified, that is, in such a way as to subserve the life of the individual or of the race more perfectly. The modifications are of three kinds. First, the animal may learn to react more discriminatingly to objects of the class which evokes the instinctive reaction: for example, a bird, which at first instinctively pursues all butterflies, learns, through experience of the nauseous taste of one species, to refrain from pursuing members of that species and of all others which have similar markings; or again, a young lamb instinctively follows any large moving object, but shortly learns to react in this way to sheep only; and later he learns to discriminate his dam from other sheep and to follow her only. In all such cases we have to infer that the innate cognitive disposition has undergone further differentiation through experiences of success and failure, pleasure and pain.

Secondly, the animal may learn to react with one of its instinctive modes of behaviour to an object of a kind towards which it at first remained indifferent. Abundant illustrations of this mode of adaptation of instinctive behaviour are provided by instances in which animals learn to devour objects other than those which they instinctively seek. The tiger, for example, does not instinctively prey upon man; but if, driven on by scarcity of food and consequent extreme hunger, he has once attacked and devoured a man, men henceforth are objects that excite his predatory impulse. Or again, a young dog does not instinctively flee in fear from a boy; but if once, or on several occasions, he has been tormented by a gang of boys, he may afterwards flee from all boys : the mere appearance of any boy may suffice to evoke the impulse of fear and its characteristic bodily expression. We have to suppose that in such cases a conative disposition becomes linked with a cognitive disposition with which it was not innately connected.

The third type of modification of instinctive behaviour consists in a modification of the bodily activities that are directed upon the object of the instinct. This is seldom exemplified except in conjunction with modification of one or other of the preceding types, or under the teaching of man. When seagulls learn to follow a ship and to snatch up pieces of food thrown overboard, or to follow the plough and feed on worms and grubs, we have an instance of modification of the mixed type ; and some of the tricks learnt by animals, such as the pushing up of a latch, provide examples of predominantly motor adaptation. Such modification of any purely instinctive mode of bodily movement implies differentiation of the innate conative disposition comprised in the instinct.

When the behaviour of an animal exhibits modification of a purely instinctive mode of behaviour of any one of these three kinds, we say that it has profited by experience and behaves intelligently. All animal behaviour is, then, either purely instinctive or intelligent ; and, when we say intelligent, we mean that it is such as implies some degree of modification of the innate structure of the mind through experience of success or failure, pleasure or pain, in the course of purposive activity. Intelligent behaviour thus always involves modification of instinctive modes of behaviour, and intelligence presupposes instinct : for, unless a creature possessed instincts of some kind, all basis for the play of intelligence would be lacking, there would be no tendencies to be modified ; and modification of pre-existing tendencies is the essence of intelligent activity.

This, then, is the relation of intelligence to instinct in the animal world ; each animal is natively endowed with certain instincts which lead it to react in specific ways to certain situations or objects of its environment ; in the course of the striving to which it is thus prompted, it may learn to modify its bodily movements, to discriminate more nicely between the objects which yield more or less of satisfaction to its impulses, or directly to

F

respond with specifically directed impulses to objects which do not normally evoke them prior to such modification ; and in proportion as an animal effects much or little of such adaptive modification of its instincts, we say that it exhibits much or little intelligence.

Now the higher animals, that is, those whose behaviour exhibits the greatest complexity and nicety of adjustment to a variety of situations, fall into two great classes ; namely, the class in which behaviour is predominantly instinctive, in which the modifications of the innate tendencies are relatively few and slight, but in which these innate tendencies are themselves very complex and highly specialized ; and, secondly, the class in which the instinctive tendencies are of low degree of specialization, but become greatly modified and specialized in various ways in the course of the individual's experience. The former class is best represented by the higher insects ; the second by the higher vertebrate animals, especially the mammals.

It is as though Nature had tried two different plans for securing the nice adjustment of her children's behaviour. The one plan is to provide in the innate mental structure of each animal as complete as possible a system of highly specialized instincts, which shall fit the creature so fully for its special environment that it has little need to modify in any way its instinctive modes of behaviour in order to thrive and propagate its kind. This is the plan usually realized in those creatures which, like most of the insects, are launched full-grown to lead an independent life of active movement ; for, if such creatures had to learn to modify extensively their innate modes of behaviour in order to cope effectively with their environment, most of them would inevitably perish before they had achieved this task.

The other plan is to provide in the innate mental structure of each animal a number of very general instincts, that is, instincts of which both the cognitive and the conative parts are but little specialized, so that the creature reacts in a few highly general ways to a corresponding number of large classes of objects ; and to supplement these instincts with a large capacity for intelligent adaptation of behaviour, through the exercise of which the innate dispositions may become specialized and differentiated to cope with a large variety of objects and circumstances. It is a necessary part of this plan that the young animal shall not, during the first period of its active life, be dependent altogether upon its own efforts ; for its highly general instincts would hardly suffice to maintain it alive unaided. Rather it must enjoy a period of sheltered life, during which it may acquire, through experience, such specializations of its innate mental structure as are necessary for independent existence. This period of protected immaturity Nature provides by developing in the species the parental instinct, which leads the adults of each generation to feed, protect, and shelter their young, while these add to their highly general innate knowledge a sufficient store of acquired knowledge.

We use here the term " innate knowledge " in referring to all that part of the structure of the mind which is inherited, in order to mark the view that it is of essentially the same nature as what we call acquired knowledge ; and this is in conformity with general usage, for by knowledge we mean the capacity to think and act in certain ways. We say that a person knows how to swim or to shoot, as well as that he knows the multiplication table, the French language, or the principles of chemistry ; and we say with equal propriety that the bee knows how to build the honey-comb, that the squirrel knows how to find and to open nuts, that the spider knows how to repair her web, or that the bird knows its own nest ; for in each case, whether the knowledge be innate or acquired, its possession consists in the presence of more or less specialized dispositions appropriately related to the rest of the structure of the mind.

When we compare these two great plans according to which adjustment of behaviour is secured, it seems obvious that the second offers the greater possibilities. Upon the former plan, the more highly specialized are the instincts of any creature and the more perfectly they are organized at the moment it enters upon its life of free activity, the less chance has it of acquiring new knowledge or of further elaborating in any way the structure of its mind ; for the highly specialized instincts, coming at once into operation, become set or confirmed by use ; and the creature is thenceforward condemned to a life of routine repetition of its purely instinctive modes of behaviour.

The second plan, on the other hand, seems to offer a prospect of unlimited possibilities of individual mental development ; for the less specialized are the instincts and the more prolonged the period of youth or protected immaturity, the more opportunity has each individual of further elaborating the structure of his mind by his own efforts. This second plan inevitably brings a further very great advantage to the species among which it obtains ; namely, it enables the acquired knowledge or experience of each generation to be in some degree handed on to the next ; that is to say, it introduces the principle of tradition. For the young animals, remaining under the care of their parents, inevitably profit in some degree by imitating their behaviour : whereas, under the other plan, the parent, having deposited the egg, is no more concerned for its welfare ; and the young, therefore, never enjoy the companionship of their parents and have no opportunity of imitating them.

The simplest way in which the young take to themselves knowledge acquired by their parents, is to follow them about and thus to learn where best to find food and shelter. But the possibilities of advantage from imitation are so great that special adaptations of innate mental structure have been evolved in many species, in order that these advantages may be more fully secured. The typical and most obvious and, perhaps, the simplest example of such special innate provision for securing to each generation the fuller benefits of family and social life, is the development of a special cognitive disposition for the perception of the expressions of fear made by other members of the species, and its innate linkage with the conative disposition in which the impulse of fear arises. In virtue of such a special development of the cognitive side of this instinct, the young bird crouches motionless or runs to shelter when the parent emits a cry of fear ; the young rabbit runs to earth when its mother's white tail bobs before it ; and among the gregarious mammals similar signals recall the young to the herd, as it prepares for collective flight or defence. The frequency among the higher animals of recognition-marks (of which the white underside of the rabbit's tail is a simple example) affords some indication of the importance of this principle. But among the higher animals the part played by tradition, through imitation of the old by the young, goes far beyond these simple modes ; thus the forms of the nests and of the songs of many birds seem to be only in part instinctively determined and in part traditionally.

If now we apply all the foregoing principles of animal behaviour to the elucidation of the relation of the human to the animal mind, the human mind appears as the product of an extreme evolution according to the second of the two great plans of mental organization. The human being necessarily inherits certain instincts ; for without these he would lack all means of setting to work on his task of building up the immense mass of acquired knowledge that he needs : that is to say, if he were not provided by heredity with some cognitive and conative dispositions, and if certain of these were not innately linked, there would be no means of setting his mental faculties to work. But his acquisition of knowledge is rapid and extensive ; for his conditions are very favourable to such acquisition. First, the instincts he inherits are of the most highly general type on both their cognitive and conative sides ; they merely provide a basis for vaguely directed activities in response to vaguely discriminated impressions from large classes of objects. Secondly, the duration of his immaturity and the period of parental protection are very greatly prolonged ; for, whereas the youth of the more intelligent animals lasts only some months, or at the most, a very few years, as in the families of the elephants and man-like apes, human beings enjoy immaturity and parental protection during nearly a score of years. Thirdly, the possibilities of profiting by tradition are immensely increased for man by his power of speech ; for language enables each generation to hand on to its successor a vastly greater store of acquired knowledge than can be transmitted in any other way ; and, of course, the invention of writing has again immensely increased the possible mass of traditional knowledge. These three favourable conditions of development of the human mind go far to explain how it attains so vast a superiority to that of the highest animal.

The study of animal behaviour, besides throwing light on the general nature of the innate basis of the human mind and on the general conditions of its development in the individual, helps us to elucidate its innate basis in detail, in that it affords us guidance when we seek to define the human instincts. For it becomes clear that, as the theory of continuous evolution demands, the human mind is endowed with a number of instincts which are very similar to some found in the higher animals; for example, the instincts of fear, of sex, and of pugnacity. While these are displayed in simple and unmistakable forms of behaviour among the animals, their operation in human beings is so largely modified and obscured by acquired modifications and the power of self-conscious control, that without the analogy presented by animal behaviour the task of defining the human instincts would be one of extreme difficulty.

The third way, we said, in which the study of animal behaviour illuminates the central problems of psychology is to show us the general nature and course of the evolution of which the human mind is the supreme achievement. We must pass over this great topic with a very few words.

We have already seen how the process of evolution has produced in its higher stages two great divergent types of mental structure ; one of the two great lines of progress seems to have culminated in the higher insects, the other and more successful line has produced man. Now, when we contemplate the behaviour of animals, representing both of these divergent lines of evolution, and that of the more lowly creatures, representing the common stem from which the lines diverge, we are led to see the unity of type of all animal behaviour ; for we note everywhere, as its characteristic marks, purposiveness, selectivity, and adaptation through experience. We are thus led to recognize the same fundamental mental faculties as operative at all levels of the evolutionary scale, but operating with very different degrees of efficiency according to the degree of development of mental structure. In this way we reach the conclusion that mental evolution has been essentially a continuous evolution of mental structure, rather than a process marked at various levels by the sudden irruption of new faculties.

Another important truth, brought home to us by this line of study, is that progressive evolution has been primarily an evolution of mental structure and only secondarily one of bodily structure. For everywhere we find the bodily structure adapting itself to the mode of life and environment of the animal. When the mammal takes to seeking its food in the water, it acquires many of the bodily peculiarities of a fish, becoming a whale or a porpoise ; when the reptile or the mammal learns to seek its prey in the air, its bodily structure approximates to that of a bird ; when the water-breather learns to come on to the land, he loses his gills and acquires lungs ; and so in thousands of cases : the change of mode of life or of behaviour leads to change of bodily structure. But the change of behaviour is the expression of a change of mental structure. Other changes of habitat and consequent changes of bodily structure, colour, and so forth, conform to the same principle : either the species is forced into a new habitat, or, owing to some change in its mental constitution, seeks a new environment ; and in both cases the individuals of each generation adapt their behaviour as best they can to the new environment, while the bodily structure gradually follows suit. Thus, mental evolution leads the way, and evolution of bodily structure is in the main the consequence of it ; and this remains true, no matter what theory of the conditions of evolution we adopt.

Unlike Darwin, most of the biologists of the present day leave the mental powers out of account altogether, when they seek to account for biological evolution ; but if it is primarily a mental evolution this procedure is doomed to failure. And the hopelessness of such mindless biology may be deduced in another way. Evolution, so far as we can at present see, has been brought about either through the transmission from one generation to another of the structural effects of the efforts of creatures at more complete adaptation to their environment ; or by the natural selection of the so-called spontaneous variations, in the course of the unremitting struggle for existence to which we all, men and animals alike, are committed ; or, more probably, by both processes. In either case the work of the mind has been an all-important condition of such evolution ; for, even if natural selection of spontaneous variations has been the sole method of evolution, such selection was only rendered possible by the struggling for existence, that is, by the sustained purposive efforts of the animals to maintain their own lives and to propagate their species. Animal evolution, that is to say, however it may have been with plant evolution, has been the product of the struggles of the animals, of their purposive efforts to survive ; for the factor determining survival or destruction in chief measure has always been success or failure of the purposive activity of the animal ; to this all other factors have been subordinate. Thus the main stress, the brunt of the work of evolution, has been borne by the mind ; the mind has been the pioneer of bodily evolution ; the bodily organs and functions have been merely the instruments through which the mind has accomplished its purposes.

We see, then, how distorted is any view of the evolutionary process which represents mind as a mere by-product of its later stages ; first coming into being, when the physical processes within the nervous systems of animals reached a certain degree of complexity. Yet that is a view of mental evolution which has been widely entertained.

Before leaving this topic, it must be pointed out that in the study of animal behaviour lies our best, perhaps our only, hope of answering the question—Are acquired characters transmitted ? Are the adaptations of behaviour and the consequent modifications of structure (bodily or mental) achieved by the efforts of individuals, transmitted in any degree to their progeny ? This is the most urgent and practically important biological problem, perhaps the most important of all problems, a definite answer to which we may confidently hope to obtain by the methods of empirical science.

Biologists have been divided into two acutely opposed parties by this question, ever since doubt was thrown on such transmission ; the majority denying it dogmatically, a strong minority as confidently affirming it. So long as we have no positive answer to this question, there can be no progress made with many of the major problems of biology and of sociology, and a wise decision on some of the most far-reaching legislative and administrative problems is wholly impossible. For example, the solution of the eugenic problem, the practical problem of promoting the progress of the human race, or of any section of it, or of preventing its deterioration, hangs upon the answer to this question. It is difficult for us to view this problem dispassionately in relation to ourselves ; let us, therefore, consider it for a moment in relation to the negro race, in order to bring home to our minds its vast importance. It seems indisputable that the negro race is, in certain respects, at a lower level of mental evolution than the white race ; now, if acquired characters are transmitted, even in a very slight degree only, we may reasonably hope that, after the negro race shall have been subjected to the better influences of civilization for a number of generations, it will be raised to a higher level of innate intellectual and moral capacity. If, on the other hand, acquired characters are not in any degree transmitted, as the majority of biologists assert, then there is no hope that the civilization and education of the negro peoples, no matter how wisely and beneficently the work may be directed, will of themselves raise them to a higher level of innate capacity. It is clear, then, that our hopes and our practical policy in relation to the negro race (and to all other races of mankind) must be profoundly affected by the establishment of the true answer to this question.

For a whole generation at least this question has been pressing for an answer, and no progress has been made with it. Yet if a tenth, or even a hundredth, part of the money which is devoted to research in physical science, in order to add to our material comforts and conveniences, could be diverted to promote the study of animal behaviour, this problem could be rapidly solved. For there is every reason to believe that the answer to it which is true of the animals is true also of man

CHAPTER VI

THE STUDY OF CHILDHOOD, AND INDIVIDUAL
PSYCHOLOGY

WE have seen in a previous chapter that the experimental methods of observation are being applied to a great variety of psychological problems, and to none more energetically than to those which are of immediate importance from the educational point of view. Many of these experimental observations are made by and upon children, especially such experiments as can be carried on collectively with a considerable group of subjects. Much of the work of this sort has been directed to the elucidation of very special problems. But the study of children has also its bearings on the wider and more general problems of the mind and its development. It has been rendered far more fruitful of results than it otherwise could have been by the light thrown by the theory of organic evolution and by the principle of recapitulation—the principle, namely, that in the course of his development each individual recapitulates or retraces, however roughly and imperfectly, the steps by which his species was evolved. In the light of this theory and of this principle, it has become obvious that the development of the mind of the child, far from being a mere moulding of it by the impressions rained upon it by its environment, is itself a process of evolution in the proper sense of the word, an unfolding of latent potentialities. In other words, we have learnt that, though education may do much, heredity is all-important ; and that education can but refine, perfect, or restrain the native tendencies of the mind. The greatest problem for the solution of which we have to rely largely on the study of children may, then, be stated as follows :—What is the nature of the mental inheritance of the normal man ? What powers, faculties, tendencies, or mental structures, does he inherit ? What is the natural order or sequence of their evolution ? The importance, both practical and theoretical, of finding the answers to these questions, is equalled by the difficulty of the task.

A part of the mental inheritance of the normal man can be roughly defined with some confidence, and the natural order of its evolution can be stated in general terms. This part consists of the human instincts. These, as in other animal species, seem to be common to the whole human race. The recognition of their presence and of their several natures is rendered difficult, first, by their highly general character ; secondly, by the fact that most of them mature, or come into operation, only when the individual has made some considerable intellectual progress ; thirdly, by the great development in man of the power of control and modification of the instinctive tendencies, or, in other words, by the complex interaction of the conative tendencies which results from the high complexity of the mental organization. The main phases of the development of the child are determined by the successive ripening of these instincts. The one which generally produces the profoundest effects— effects which make themselves felt throughout wellnigh the whole of the mental life—is the sex instinct. Whether this is normally operative in any degree before the onset of puberty is an obscure question on which opinions differ widely ; but it is clear that it either first comes into operation at puberty, or becomes much more powerfully operative at that time ; and it is clear also that the profound bodily and mental changes which characterize that period of life are largely due to its evolution. The very great influence upon the course of mental life which is often exercised by it, is due not only to the great strength of the impulse to which its excitement gives rise, but also to the fact that it begins to exert its strong influence at a time when the rest of the mind has attained a high level of development, when

self-consciousness has already become highly
elaborated, and when the individual has
already formed a complex system of sentiments and habits and has entered into a
complex system of social relations ; for the
awakening of this new impulse, however blind
it may remain, necessitates profound read-
justments of all these acquisitions, and affects
profoundly many judgments of value and
many emotional attitudes.   For these reasons
the period of puberty is of critical importance,
and the study and understanding of it are
an imperative necessity to the educator.   But
this instinct is only first in strength and
influence among others ; and the obvious
importance of the study of it serves to make
us appreciate the need for the definition and
understanding of other powerful instincts,
and of the course of their evolution in the
human being.

When we turn to ask—What besides the
instincts is comprised in the innate constitution of the human mind ? we find the widest
divergences of opinion and the greatest
difficulty in returning any answer.   What we
have called the mental faculties are, of course,
inherited.   But does the inheritance include
anything more than these and the instincts ?
If we are right in saying that any mind can be
wholly described in terms of its faculties and

its structure, we may put the question in the following form:—Does the native basis of the mind comprise any dispositions in addition to those which enter into the composition of the instincts; and, if so, to what extent are they systematically linked together?

We cannot answer this question with a negative. There is certainly much beside the faculties and the instincts comprised in the native basis of each human mind. If there were not, it would be impossible adequately to account for the vast superiority of the mind of the human adult to that of the highest of the animals. Some of those who regard the mind purely from the physiological standpoint, and who believe that all we have called the structure of the mind can be adequately described in terms of the organized structure of the brain, take the view that the superiority of the native endowment of man consists chiefly or wholly in the presence in the brain of the infant of a great mass of unorganized nervous tissue, which offers unlimited possibilities of progressive organization. But, even if we accepted the assumption that the structure of the mind can be wholly described in terms of nervous dispositions and their connexions, we could not accept the view that nothing of the mental organization beyond the instincts is innate.

We have to recognize that the greater part of what we have called the logical structure of the mind is innately given ; that is to say, that there are given the principal great cognitive systems, by means of which we implicitly think the most general properties and relations of things, in thinking of particular objects. No direct proof of the truth of this view can be offered ; but in support of it the following considerations may be advanced.

The fact that the human mind develops so far beyond the highest animal mind cannot be wholly accounted for by the more favourable conditions of its development ; of which, as we have seen, the highly general character of its instincts, prolonged youth, and the use of language as the instrument of communication and tradition, are the chief. If the superiority resulted from such conditions merely, it should be possible, by careful training, to raise the mind of an animal much nearer to the human level than it can actually be brought. As a matter of fact, the most favourable conditions and the most careful training bring the animal mind but a very little part of the way towards the human mind.

Again, the behaviour of young children affords evidence of their implicit knowledge of such things and relations as space, spatial relations, thinghood, causality, at a time when they are quite incapable of explicitly thinking of such objects, and when they can hardly be supposed to have built up such knowledge through their own experience.

But perhaps the strongest evidence is afforded by the inequalities of the intellectual and moral development, as respects both kind and degree, of children placed under similar conditions and influences. These inequalities are much greater than any that could be attributed to favouring or retarding influences. For we see sometimes a child growing up under the most unfavourable conditions of every kind, and yet rapidly and easily attaining a high level of development; and we see others under the most favourable conditions remaining stupid and of low moral level, or exhibiting special intellectual defects or moral deformities.

Again, among those children who develop exceptionally high powers, we commonly find that the development of these powers cannot be accounted for by the influences of their environments. And in many cases it is obvious that their special excellences are innate or have an innate basis; for the same peculiarities can be traced in their ancestry through several generations; they are, therefore, hereditary, and whatever is inherited is innate. The most striking instances are those in which the hereditary peculiarity takes the form of excellence (or defect) in highly special forms of mental activity, such as musical and mathematical talent ; but similar evidence of highly special innate powers and tendencies is afforded by the appearance of numberless family traits, idiosyncrasies of thought and feeling, and special mental excellences and defects of many kinds. Perhaps the most striking evidence is afforded by the study of twins, who sometimes, even though brought up under very different influences, exhibit very close resemblances of intellect and character. In short, the more children are studied from this point of view, the more far-reaching does the influence of heredity appear. Now, although it is generally impossible to define in anything but the roughest way the innate bases of these hereditary peculiarities, we seem compelled to believe that they consist —in large part at least—in inherited mental structures of very considerable degrees of specialization.

Here, then, is an immense field for research, the extent and importance of which we are only just beginning to realize. And it is a field for the psychologist. He alone can hope to define the problems in the detailed way which is the necessary presupposition of fruit-ful work in this field. This is sufficiently shown by the few attempts made to enter it by biologists and statisticians without psychological preparation. They tend to work in terms of the confused notions and crude distinctions embodied in popular speech ; they attempt to determine the inheritance of such questionable entities as good temper, courage, conscientiousness, or popularity ; ignoring the necessity of accurate psychological analysis of the constitution of the mind as the preliminary to all such work.

If education, properly understood and practised, is what the word implies, a drawing out of the native powers of the mind, a wise direction and control of the process of spontaneous development of innate tendencies, surely, when every civilized nation devotes enormous sums of money and the self-sacrificing energy of many thousands of teachers to the work of educating its children, it must be worth while to find out what are those innate tendencies and what is their normal course of development.

Individual Psychology

Individual Psychology is a field for the application of the knowledge and understanding acquired by study in the other departments of the science, rather than a branch which directly contributes towards the solution of its general problems. Its work is to define the peculiarities of mental constitution which render the behaviour and the development of each individual human being unique. Its success depends upon the degree of progress achieved by the other departments. For, before we can give an adequate account of the individual, we must be able to describe in general terms the innate basis of the mind, in so far as it is common to all men ; and we must be able to state the general principles of the development of the mind under the joint influences of its native tendencies and of its environment. In this field psychology comes near to art ; for biography, fiction, and drama are largely concerned with the portrayal of the intellectual and moral peculiarities of individuals.

It is true that at the present time the character of an individual may be more effectively displayed by the sympathetic intuition of the artist, than by the application of the rudiments of psychological science that have hitherto been built up. But, as psychology progresses, it will more and more aid in the accurate delineation of individual disposition and temperament and character ; and it will enable us, not only to portray, but also to understand and explain, them in terms of heredity and the laws of mental development.

What accurate work is being done in this

field mainly takes the form of experimental determination of capacities to execute definite tasks. The task set is of such a nature that the degree of excellence attained by the subject is capable of being accurately stated in terms of the number of some unit, units of rate, or of repetition, or of errors committed. By the application of such a " mental test " to any number of subjects under strictly similar conditions, the subjects may be placed in an order of merit in respect of excellence in the performance of the task. Now it is perhaps not possible to devise tests which can be regarded as testing any one mental function purely. It might, for example, seem an easy matter to devise a simple test for memory. But, whatever form of test is applied, at least two very different functions are involved, and the degree of excellence of each perform-ance depends on both of them—namely, the function of committing to memory, and the function of retaining that which has been committed. In a similar way every other simple experiment tests not a single function, but a complex of functions.

Nevertheless, the application of a well-chosen set of carefully devised tests to a group of subjects, say fifty or more children of the same age and school experience, is capable of throwing much light upon their relative capacities ; and, if the process is repeated at intervals of six months or a year, further light upon their individual peculiarities is obtained. Little has yet been done in this direction ; but there seems to be no reason why we should not ultimately work out a scheme of mental tests which will allow us to estimate the intellectual capacities of any individual with considerable accuracy, and to assign him his place in an empirical scale of capacity, far more accurately than can be done by any other method of examination yet devised. One great advantage of such a method of estimating intellectual capacity over our ordinary examination methods is that it should enable us to distinguish more fully the respective shares of native capacity and of acquired knowledge in the performances of any individual.

The data obtained by the application of mental tests may be made to yield further conclusions of great interest by the mathematical treatment of them according to the principle of correlation. By applying this method we can discover what kinds of excellences or defects commonly go together in the composition of the human mind. For example, we take the two lists of figures representing the achievements of a considerable group of subjects under two different tests, and arrange them in order of merit ; then, if the subjects appear approximately in the same order of merit in the two lists, we may infer that the functions involved in the two performances are correlated, *i.e.* that they tend to be of the same level of excellence in the same subjects. And if we find no such correspondence between the two lists, or if we find an inverted correspondence, those near the top of one list being near the bottom of the other ; then we may infer that there is no correlation, or a negative correlation, between the functions involved.

With this very brief indication of a method of investigation which not only promises great things for Individual Psychology, but which raises also the prospect of effecting ultimately a complete objective analysis of the mental functions, we must pass on to our next topic, namely, the study of abnormal mental processes.

CHAPTER VII

ABNORMAL PSYCHOLOGY

ABNORMAL psychology offers a vast and fascinating and, just at the present time, a very fruitful field of research. It can probably claim a much larger number of serious students

than any of the other departments, and it
excites much more popular interest than any
of them.   The ordinary man is so accustomed
to the ordinary behaviour of normal men and
to his own habitual modes of thinking, that
he cannot see behind them any problems to
be solved.   The notion of any one trying to
find out more about the human mind than he
himself knows, generally fills him with im-
patient scorn, even though he may be prepared
to tolerate those who spend their lives in
classifying beetles or minutely describing the
skeletons of microscopic animalcules.   But,
when one meets a man who gravely and
persistently asserts that his conduct is constantly governed by the voice of an invisible
being, or that he sees beside him a human figure
which none other can see, or that he is the
emperor of the world ; or when one hears of a
man who repeatedly inflicts painful mutilations
upon his own body, or who refuses to move
hand or foot for months at a time ; then even
the dullest man is startled into curiosity, and
feels himself in presence of a fact that calls
for explanation and understanding.

Abnormal psychology comprises a number
of sub-departments, which in the main have
been pursued independently by different
bodies of workers ; happily, in recent years
these groups have come more closely together

and are now giving mutual aid. We may broadly distinguish two groups of these sub-departments, namely, those that are concerned with minds in definitely morbid or pathological states, and those concerned with distinctly unusual or abnormal states of mind which cannot fairly be classed as morbid. The former group consists of two sub-departments : the study of mental diseases proper and that of the psycho-neuroses. The separation of these studies is largely conventional and professional rather than scientific, and there is manifest at the present time a strong tendency to abolish it.

Until recent years the study of mental diseases proper had in the main pursued in strange detachment from the other branches of psychology, and it had thrown but little light on the major problems of the science. This was mainly due to the prevalence among the physicians for mental diseases of a tendency to seek to understand and explain all the morbid conditions of mind in terms of structural disorder or disease of the brain only. Some mental diseases are primarily diseases of the brain, and in cases of certain types gross inflammatory or degenerative changes of the brain tissues are regularly found upon *post mortem* examination. But this fact does not justify the assumption that all mental disease is of this nature ; and of late years there has appeared a strong tendency to seek for mental or functional causes of the abnormal course of mental process in insane patients. This tendency has been greatly stimulated by the modern developments of the other department of mental pathology. In this second department the disease which provides the largest number of patients and the most interesting material for the student of psychology is hysteria.

A generation ago the attitude of the medical profession towards hysteria and allied abnormal conditions was, with very few exceptions, wholly unscientific, being based merely on popular psychology. It was vaguely recognized that the extraordinary behaviour of the hysterical patient implied some kind of mental abnormality, and that no gross disease of the nervous system was implied by it. But the tendency then prevalent may be crudely described by saying that the abnormal behaviour of the hysteric was attributed to " pure cussedness " ; the treatment accorded was " firmness ", strong electric shocks, cold douches, and other decorous substitutes for a sound birching. To a small group of French physicians belongs in the main the credit of having put the study of hysteria and allied conditions on a scientific basis, by showing that the patients must be regarded as suffering from a disorder of mental origin and must be treated in the main through the mind. They succeeded in showing that in many such cases, perhaps in all, the essence of the disorder is some division of the mind into parts which, instead of co-operating in normal fashion, function more or less independently of one another and even enter into some sort of rivalry. It was shown that, while in the majority of cases the division takes the form of the separation of some minor functions only, in others there occurs something like a separation of functions into two rival systems that compete with one another for the control of behaviour, sometimes the one, sometimes the other predominating ; and it was shown that more rarely such rival systems seem to maintain their activities simultaneously, the behaviour of the patient seeming to express at any one moment the purposes of two minds. In this way was introduced the notion of the division or splitting of the personality, resulting in alternating or in coexistent dual personalities. Of these two conceptions that of alternating personalities is the clearer and more intelligible. Under it are generally classed rare cases of the type which in former ages was explained as due to " possession " of the body of the patient by a

" demon " or by the spirit of some deceased person.

In a typical well-marked case of this sort, the patient's normal life suddenly gives way to a period in which he behaves in a manner altogether " unlike himself." He wanders perhaps to some distant place, and there takes up some new mode of life under a new name, behaving sufficiently like a normal person to avoid the attention of the police or of the medical profession. After weeks, months, or years of the new mode of life, he suddenly changes again, perhaps waking up one morning to find that his surroundings are wholly strange to him, and that he remembers nothing of his past life from the moment at which he left home ; in short, he becomes himself again, after being to all intents and purposes a different person. Thereafter he may relapse at longer or shorter intervals into the secondary state, " coming to himself " again after each period of secondary existence. In the greater number of such cases, each of the two alternating personalities has no direct knowledge of the other or of his doings, the period of the dominance of the one being a complete blank for the memory of the other ; and the two personalities commonly differ widely in respect to temperament.

It is attempted to render such cases intelligible by pointing out that most of us experience from time to time changes similar in kind, though much less in degree ; for example, one passes into a mood in which all one's thinking has an unusual emotional tone, say, a tone of melancholy ; and so long as this tone prevails, one dwells upon gloomy memories, forgetting the brighter phases of one's past life, one's thinking reaches pessimistic conclusions, and one's behaviour reveals this inward gloom. Now, it is said, imagine this condition to be accentuated and recurrent, and you have an approximation to alternation of personalities ; the border-line being crossed when the emotional tones of the alternating periods become so widely different that in each period the memories only of the periods of congruent tone are recoverable.

The cases of dual personality of the concurrent type are rarely so extreme. The existence of a secondary personality is inferred from certain features of the behaviour of the bodily organism which seem to bear no relation to the thinking of the subject, so far as he can reveal it to us ; for example, the patient has an anæsthetic or insensitive arm and hand, and this can be induced to write intelligible answers to questions whispered in his ear, while the subject, who afterwards denies all knowledge of both question and answer, maintains an animated conversation with a third person. Or the anæsthetic hand may be pricked a given number of times, and, though the subject remains, so far as can be ascertained, unaware that the hand has been touched, the hand itself may be induced to write down the number of the pricks.

In such cases, according to the commonly received view, the impressions made on the anæsthetic limb fail to affect the thinking of the subject, but evoke instead a feeble trickle of mental activity, which flows on as an independent subsidiary stream alongside the main stream ; since this main stream is, as it were, deprived of the influence of these sense-impressions, the lesser stream is said to have been split off from the greater. The facts are interpreted after the analogy of a river which overflows its banks at one spot, and thus sends off a small divergent stream which follows for a time a separate course.

In the rarest and most interesting of all these strange cases of dual personality, the phenomena of the alternating and the concurrent types are presented by the same organism. During the dominance of the normal personality, a secondary personality reveals itself occasionally in the production of movements of which the normal personality remains unconscious or for which he denies all responsibility, and which yet express intelligent appreciation of the circumstances of the moment ; and later, when the secondary personality is dominant, he claims to remember the incident and to have willed the " automatic " movements.

In face of such puzzling cases, some of which have been studied with the most admirable patience and acumen by the French physicians, and also more recently by some American doctors, any hypothesis must be put forward tentatively. The view that they all imply or result from some kind of division of the mental functions into two systems which carry on their activities independently of one another—this view finds support in many facts (though others cannot easily be reconciled with it), and is widely accepted. But this view is really nothing more than a hypothetical description of the condition, and needs to be supplemented by some hypothesis which will explain the production of the condition. Such an hypothesis is that of Professor Janet, to whom more than to any other our present knowledge of these states is due. He assumes that the unity of the mind, as normally revealed in the direction of its activity towards one topic at any one moment, is conditioned by the exercise of a synthetic power or energy which is one of the fundamental functions or faculties of mind ; and he supposes that, in the patients who exhibit these curious modes of behaviour, this synthetic energy is for one reason or another defective ; hence, he says, the mind cannot perform so completely as the normal mind its unifying function, and its activities, instead of being harmonized in one stream which, however broad and deep, is nevertheless a single complex activity, fall apart into two or even more streams, with the result that the patient's field of consciousness or stream of mental activity is narrowed and that indications of subconscious activities appear.

In recent years our knowledge of this group of pathological states of mind has been further enriched by the work of Prof. Freud of Vienna, who also has sought to carry further the theoretical explanation of them by means of a system of ingenious hypotheses. At the present time these hypotheses are by no means generally accepted, but are the subject of a most lively and heated controversy ; nevertheless, they are so well supported by the good results obtained by many physicians who have applied them in the treatment of patients, and their interest from the point of view of the major problems of psychology is so great, that some indication of their nature must be given here.

The French conception of hysteria tends to be intellectualistic ; *i.e.* it takes but little account of the function of will or conation in mental life. In the teaching of Freud a leading rôle is assigned to conation. The fundamental fact from which the theory starts out is that our organized conative tendencies are apt to come into conflict with one another, producing what we called moral struggles. Every case of what is commonly called temptation involves such a conflict of conative tendencies ; when, in such a conflict, we conquer our temptation, our highly organized self-consciousness brings into operation a strongly organized system of conative tendencies which support the more moral or social tendency in its conflict with the immoral or socially disapproved tendency, and thus secure the defeat of the latter. Now, we know that such a defeated tendency, or conquered temptation, is not always destroyed or wholly abolished by such a victory of one's moral nature in open conflict ; we know that in some cases it recurs and requires to be thrust down again and again. But in many cases we succeed, either at once or after repeated conflicts, in banishing this temptation from consciousness. We commonly feel then that we have done with it and wholly cast it out or destroyed it. Now, it is possible or even

ABNORMAL PSYCHOLOGY 199

probable that, when we stoutly face a temptation, frankly recognizing it for what it is, an expression of a lower possibility of our nature, a conative tendency opposed to our moral sentiments, and when we thus conquer it, the tendency is destroyed. But it seems (and this is the essential novelty in Freud's teaching) that many natures, especially perhaps women brought up in a strictly conventional manner, react in a different way to their temptations; they are so horrified at the first dim awareness of the nature of their temptation that they never frankly recognize it, never bring it out into the light in order to confront it in open conflict. The tendency is apt then to be repressed and yet to live and work in the mind in a subterraneous fashion; it becomes, as it were, a parasitic growth seeking constantly to force its way to consciousness, or, in other words, to determine the conscious thinking of the subject. But the subject's moral nature, being radically opposed to it, maintains a rigid censorship, again in a subconscious fashion; and so there goes on a perpetual subterranean or subconscious conflict. In states of diminished mental alertness, as in dreaming or mere day-dreaming, this repression, maintained by the organized system of tendencies which constitute the moral nature, is liable to partial remission;

it becomes less effective, and then the repressed tendency finds its chance to determine the subject's conscious thinking. Even in such states, it commonly fails to express itself directly and clearly in the course of the subject's thinking, but rather finds expression only in symbolical fashion. Thus, in the dreams of such a person, the repressed tendency is apt to manifest itself in a flight of imagery which, when described by the dreamer, may seem to have no relation to the repressed tendency, and which is not recognized by the dreamer as so related, but which in reality symbolizes the course of events subconsciously desired by him. In this way, it is held, the tendency achieves a certain measure of the satisfaction which in the waking state is wholly denied to it by the rigid censorship of the moral nature.

Such analysis and interpretation of dreams occupies a very important position in Freud's system of psycho-pathology; for it was a main point of departure from which the whole system was developed; and it discovers an analogy between the dream-experiences of normal persons and the processes which are assumed to underlie and express themselves in the symptoms of hysteria. It has, therefore, been much criticized; but there can be little doubt that, though some of its most enthusiastic exponents have gone too far in asserting that every dream is determined by the subconscious working of a repressed tendency, such interpretation does in some cases hit the mark and reveal a wealth of subconscious mental activity of which the dream is the expression in consciousness.

It may be objected—How is it possible to establish any such interpretation ?—How can it be more than guesswork ? To this the reply is that the interpretation is achieved by an intricate process of delicate analysis ; and, though this process opens the door to many possibilities of error, yet on the whole the analysis of a very large number of dreams, by various observers who have used this method, has revealed a certain lawfulness and consistency of mode of operation which forbid us to set aside the interpretations as purely arbitrary ; and further, they are borne out by the analogous processes revealed as issuing in the symptoms of hysterical patients.

The symptoms of the hysteric take the form not only of perverted modes of thinking, such as the baseless conviction of having performed some reprehensible action, or other troublesome obsessions ; but also very commonly that of the performance of seemingly senseless actions, of paralysis of various organs, legs, arms, organs of speech, and so forth ; and

of anæsthesia or complete insensitiveness of
parts of the skin or of other sense-organs.
Now, according to the doctrine of Freud, these
symptoms also are, like the perverted course
of thinking and like the thinking of the
dreamer, symbolical expressions of repressed
tendencies. We have to suppose that in
the normal person the mental forces which
maintain the repression suffice to prevent any
expression of the tendency save in dreams, or
in reverie, or in occasional bodily movements
which seem to be senseless and accidental ; but
that in certain persons, whose mental energy is
depressed either by violent emotional shock,
by long-continued excess of work, or by the
persistent subconscious conflict between the
repressed tendency and the moral nature, the
repressing forces fail to accomplish their task
in an adequate manner ; so that the tendency
succeeds in asserting itself more fully, though
still in a symbolical or indirect manner only.
The symptoms of the hysterical patient thus
appear as so many disguises, adopted by a
repressed tendency in order to evade the
censorship of the moral nature and to obtain
a partial satisfaction through playing some
part in the determination of conscious thought
and of behaviour.

A relatively simple type of such indirect
expression of a repressed tendency, which

may serve to illustrate the principle, is the recurrent hallucinatory perception of some object. The object thus falsely perceived is found in some cases to be one with which the patient happened to be employed at the moment of some emotional crisis in the course of the moral conflict that resulted in repression ; such an object has no intrinsic connexion with the tendency, and the occasion of the perception of it may have escaped the conscious memory of the patient ; and, just for this reason it would seem, it is seized upon by the repressed tendency as a means of evading the censorship and securing a secret satisfaction. In a classical instance of this type recorded by Freud, the patient complained of perceiving almost constantly a strong odour of burnt pudding. Of this hallucination she could suggest no explanation ; yet it was ultimately found that, at a moment of emotional crisis in the history of a repressed love attraction, she had been occupied with a burnt pudding.

Now, as of the interpretation of dreams, the reader properly and naturally asks— What proof can be given of the correctness of such interpretation of symptoms ? The answer is twofold ; first, when by a long and delicate process of analysis the physician has discovered a repressed tendency and its probable connexion with such a symptom, the patient frequently remembers the circumstances which determined the form of the symptom and recognizes the significance attributed to it ; secondly, it appears that in many cases, when the patient has been led to recognize frankly the nature of the tendency which has been repressed, to face it courageously, and to bring the whole history of it under the free criticism of his intellectual and moral nature, all the symptoms rapidly disappear and the patient is restored to health.

A useful confirmation of the reality of the subconscious operation of conative tendencies has been provided by the application of a very simple experimental procedure to both normal and abnormal subjects. If a list of words is called aloud to any subject, he having been instructed to reply to each one by calling aloud some other word with the least possible delay, he will reply to most of the words after a delay whose duration is not more than one or two seconds ; but in any considerable list of words so applied, there are usually a few to which his reaction is longer delayed or in some other respect abnormal. And it is found, in nearly all such cases, that the word in question has some emotional significance, or that the object denoted is connected in the mind of the subject with some strong conative tendency, often one more or less repressed.

Enough, perhaps, has been said to suggest the nature of this new system of ideas, and to indicate their value and significance. It is sometimes asked—What has psychology done to enable us to benefit in any way our fellow-men? Much might be said in reply to this question, but perhaps the most striking answer would be to point to a number of men and women, who, after being for many years a painful burden to themselves and their friends, and after having been subjected without benefit to many forms of medical treatment, have been restored to health and happiness and usefulness by the application of psychological knowledge and psychological theory. This new doctrine and the practice based upon it are of importance not only in the one province of medicine in which they have been worked out; their interest and importance go far beyond those limits. They are leading to a great extension of the psychological attitude towards mental diseases of all kinds; and they are opening vistas of great extensions of our knowledge of the workings of the normal mind; especially they are revealing a realm of subconscious mental activity the existence of which had been vaguely conjectured, but which had remained unexplored and altogether problematical. For both the continued repression of the reprehensible tendencies, and the processes by which they partially evade control, are distinctly purposive activities ; and the latter seem to involve in some cases complex and subtle operations. And, if the interpretation of dreams according to this new method is not altogether fanciful, some complex dreams are not, as hitherto generally assumed, merely fortuitous and purposeless streams of pictorial fancies ; rather, they are full at every point of significance, are in fact highly elaborated trains of symbolical imagery produced by ingeniously selective and constructive thinking, which, while remaining subconscious, is guided and sustained by a hidden purpose or design.

If the symptoms of the hysteric, and the imagery that fills the consciousness of the dreamer, are the products of elaborate though subconscious mental activity, we may fairly suppose that the waking thoughts of the normal man may be in part the expression of similar subconscious activities ; and Freud and his followers are actively carrying their principles into many fields of normal psychology, and especially are applying them to throw light upon the genesis of works of art and literature. In this way morbid psychology is being brought into fruitful relations both with normal psychology and with the study of mental states and processes that are abnormal without being morbid.

These latter constitute a wide field of study which can only be negatively defined by saying that it comprises all states and processes that are neither normal nor morbid. It may be roughly divided into two parts, that of the subnormal and that of the supernormal. The former comprises such states as idiocy and weak-mindedness, and alcoholic and other intoxications in so far as they involve impairment of mental processes. These are not without their own special interest, but they cannot compete in this respect with the supernormal manifestations ; for in dealing with this division we are constantly confronted by the problem of the future evolution of the human mind, and we seem to get glimpses of immense possibilities, of modes of mental operation and communication indefinitely transcending the recognized limits of the usual and the normal. The principal topics of this field may be grouped under the following heads :—

(1) Subconscious operations producing results similar to those of normal thinking ; (2) supernormal manifestations in the domains of intellect and character, including the production of works of genius, religious con-

version, and mystical experiences ; (3) super-normal influence of the mind over the body ; (4) supernormal processes of communication between mind and mind.

The phenomena falling under all these heads are connected by the fact that all of them seem to imply more or less extensive subconscious operations ; and it has been attempted to bring them all under one explanation by the hypothesis that each of us has a twofold mental constitution and a double mental life ; namely, the normal life of conscious thought conditioned by one of the two constitutions, and the subconscious mental life conditioned by a second more or less independent mind or department of the mind. Various names, such as the " subliminal self," the " subconscious mind," the " secondary self," and so forth, have been applied to this hypothetical department of the mind. Now, it cannot be too strongly laid down, in view of the popularity of these catchwords, that, as commonly used, they are little or nothing more than words that serve to cloak our ignorance and to disguise from ourselves the need for further investigation. For the ordinary procedure is to postulate a " subconscious mind,". and then merely to assign to its agency all the varied phenomena of a supernormal character, its nature remaining completely undefined and its capacities for the production of marvels being regarded as without limit in any direction.

It is, of course, a legitimate enterprise to attempt to work out an hypothesis of this sort ; but we must recognize that none has yet been devised which can claim to be a satisfactory working hypothesis by which the facts can be brought into intelligible order. We must recognize also that the relations of subconscious operations to conscious thinking are in many cases so intimate, so much of the nature of participation in the working out of a single purpose, that any such division of the mind into two unlike parts, such as is commonly implied by names of the kind mentioned above, appears wholly unwarranted. We shall, therefore, do well to consider the supernormal phenomena under some such provisional classification as that suggested above, without committing ourselves to any hypothesis which attributes them all to any one special agency or entity.

(1) The evidence of subconscious operations producing results similar to those of normal thinking is abundant. It is obtainable experimentally in unlimited quantities by hypnotic and post-hypnotic suggestion. Hypnosis is an artificially induced condition of partial quiescence of the mind, allied to

sleep. After a long period of unscientific dogmatic denial, the scientific world at last recognizes that this condition can be induced in the great majority of normal persons, and that it is in itself perfectly harmless. It is now recognized also that hypnotism (the study of hypnosis) opens many problems of the greatest interest and provides methods for investigating them. By means of it, many of the peculiarities of mental process characteristic of hysteria and other pathological states, and many of the supernormal phenomena, can be experimentally produced and studied ; and it provides effective methods of treating many disorders in the production or maintenance of which a nervous or a mental factor plays a part.

In the present connexion the facts of post-hypnotic suggestion claim our attention. Any good subject may be told, while in the hypnotic state, to perform some simple action at some definite time or upon some signal being given ; and, if then awakened before the appointed moment, he will carry out the suggestion, although he cannot remember in the interval or immediately after performing the action, even if closely questioned, what suggestion was given him. And the signal may be of such a nature that its appreciation involves mental activity of considerable complexity ; for example, the subject may be told that he will open and shut the door when the observer touches his own face with his left hand for the eleventh time. In such a case (and the experiment may be varied and complicated indefinitely with the best subjects) the subject in some sense watches the operator, notes and counts the significant movements, and carries out the suggestion ; and yet he truthfully denies that he was aware of the nature of the command given, or of the fact that the observer had touched his face even once ; and in some cases the subject cannot even remember his execution of the suggested action immediately after its performance. Here, then, is indisputable and abundant evidence that a train of purposive mental activity, which controls to some extent the behaviour of the subject, may go on while he is consciously thinking of other matters.

Another and equally striking kind of evidence of the same fact is afforded by "automatic" writing, an accomplishment which a certain number of normal persons are capable of acquiring. In an ordinary case of this kind the subject may sit reading or talking, while his hand, holding a pencil upon a writing-block, writes more or less coherent and intelligible passages of prose or verse, of which he remains ignorant until, like any other person, he reads the script. In various closely analogous ways other automatic movements may reveal guidance which is indisputably intelligent and yet independent of the conscious thinking of the subject ; popular methods of inducing such movements are table-tilting with the finger-tips, planchette writing, and the " ouija " game. In some cases these movements reveal knowledge of facts which cannot be recalled to conscious memory ; and in others they reveal deliberate intention and ingenious design of which the subject remains unconscious. It should be added that the " automatic script " commonly consists chiefly of detached sentences or mere fragments of sentences ; yet in some cases it consists of long connected passages not without literary merit.

(2) Another type of evidence of the same class consists in the solution of problems, or the production of written matter of literary merit, during sleep or while the mind is occupied with other matters. The special interest of these cases is that they form a transition to the processes of the second class (p. 207), namely, the production of works of genius, religious conversion, and mystical experience. For there is a natural tendency to set such processes apart by themselves and to accentuate their differences from normal mental process.

But it is more conducive to an understanding of them to seek and to accentuate the points of resemblance, rather than those of difference. From this point of view we do well to begin the consideration of such facts by insisting on the large proportion of subconscious mental activity which is involved in our everyday thinking. Whoever has made on the spur of the moment a witty remark will probably be prepared on reflection to acknowledge that the words sprang to his lips without any deliberate search for them, and that the mental process, the assimilation of two seemingly unlike things, or relations, or what not, accomplished itself in secret, the result only coming to consciousness as the words issued from his lips ; and he may subsequently have found, somewhat to his surprise, that there was more in his remark than he at first realized.

This is the kind of normal activity which we may set at the lower end of a continuous scale, at the upper end of which we may place the achievement of the greatest works of genius. At every level of this scale we seem to see at work the same factors or contributing conditions, but in very different proportions. In the first place it is to be noted that the subconscious activity which is revealed by the achievement expresses in some sense the previous mental development of the subject, his interests, knowledge, and character. The dull pedant does not suddenly coruscate in flashes of wit ; the calculating prodigy does not solve problems in the higher branches of mathematics without previous study of those branches ; the person who has neither learnt to enjoy, nor been trained in the technique of, a particular art does not suddenly produce a masterpiece. Sudden conversions and mystical experiences may seem in some cases to be exceptions to this rule ; but it is doubtful whether on closer examination any such exception could be substantiated. It will usually be found that the religious convert or mystic, no matter how little his previous life may have shown the influence of religion, has been at some period of his life subjected to religious influences ; in the common phrase, the good seed has been sown and has ripened in secret.

Again, the subconscious activity usually expresses the influence of some conscious volition or conation. The problem which is solved during sleep is usually one with which the sleeper has striven while awake. Even the sudden outburst of wit implies a certain conative attitude. The sudden formulation of a great scientific hypothesis is preceded by much thinking directed to the problem. The compositions of the musician or the poet express his will to compose, often his explicit intention at the moment, but in any case a general attitude of his will. Even the automatic writer can to some extent voluntarily set himself to produce the automatic script. And religious conversion or ecstasy is usually preceded by a longing or striving for some change of life, some new mode of consciousness, though it may be little more than a vague discontent with life as hitherto known and lived. These considerations justify us in seeking to exhibit even the more extreme and extensive forms of subconscious activity as continuous with normal mental activities, rather than as processes of an altogether different order, wholly attributable to some second mind, whether a " subconscious mind " of the subject or some mind external to and altogether independent of his normal mind.

(3) The supernormal control of the mind over the bodily processes is a topic that has been brought into the forefront of popular interest of late years. Systems of mental healing, or at least methods of treating bodily disease that rely little or not at all on physical or chemical agencies, are enjoying a great vogue ; and even the medical men of this country are becoming aware that there is " something in " hypnotism, and that the

methods of suggestion and persuasion and even the claims of the " Christian Scientists " are deserving of some unbiased attention.

In all this disputed region, in which the plain man of science feels himself to be walking on a quagmire, surrounded with mists, the effects of hypnotic suggestion provide the one sure evidence that mental influences upon bodily processes may go far beyond the normal or ordinarily recognized. And this evidence forbids us to shut our eyes to the possibility that some elements of truth and reality are mixed up with the large mass of error and deception that grows up in connexion with every system of mental healing. For it shows us the reality of mental influences upon the nutrition, repair, and regulation of bodily organs, which influences nevertheless completely elude our understanding ; and it forces us to recognize that we can set no limit to the extent of such influences. It is characteristic of all or most of the methods of mental healing that, in so far as they are real, they involve mental activities which are largely subconscious.

(4) Passing now to consider supernormal communication of mind with mind, we enter a region of critical importance for our interpretation of the foregoing classes of supernormal phenomena. For if, as has always been maintained by most of the religious

systems, minds can communicate with, or in any way influence, one another in some direct fashion which does not involve the use of the organs of sense ; then we must be prepared to look outside the mind of the individual for the explanation of some at least of the supernormal manifestations of mental activity. Explanations of this sort have always been accepted by the greater part of mankind : hence the crucial importance of any positive empirical evidence of such direct communication or influence, and hence the need for the most impartial and critical examination of any evidence alleged to be of this nature. The word " telepathy " has recently come into general use to denote the direct action of mind on mind ; the crucial question may therefore be stated in the form—Does telepathy occur ? The efforts of the well-known Society for Psychical Research have for more than a generation been largely directed towards establishing an affirmative answer to this question, by means of experiments of many kinds and the collection and critical sifting of facts which seem to demand this hypothesis for their explanation. The evidence accumulated by these efforts is such as would suffice to establish the fact in dispute for all normal minds, were it not that the question is of so momentous importance.

Admitting, then, the necessity of still holding our minds in suspense on this question, let us glance at the prospect opened out by the highly probable, but not perhaps completely verified, assumption that telepathy occurs. If this assumption is accepted, the mind of the individual organism no longer appears as inevitably isolated from all other minds, or as communicating with them only by the medium of the bodily organs of expression and sense-perception ; and it is open to us to seek to explain mental processes and effects that seem otherwise inexplicable as due to the direct influence of other minds. Two distinct lines of explanation are then open to us. First, we may seek to explain certain supernormal mental processes by invoking the influence of some of those minds of which we have positive knowledge, namely, the minds of our contemporary fellow-men ; we might, for example, suppose that religious conversions, or some of the supernormal effects of mind on body, are brought about by the influence of some one stronger mind, or by the concentration of several or many minds, upon the one. But this supposition would fail to explain some of the facts and alleged facts, notably the inspirations of genius that exceed the powers of all other existing persons, and cases in which persons seem to display knowledge that was in the possession of no person living at the time.

In this way, many of those who regard some of these supernormal manifestations as inexplicable, unless the direct influence of mind on mind is assumed, are led to see in them evidence of the influence of disembodied minds. The study of abnormal psychology has thus become a field in which it is sought to find empirical evidence for two of the most ancient and widely held beliefs of the human race; namely, the belief in the survival of human personalities after bodily death, and the belief in the communion of human with divine mind.

Evidence in support of the former belief is sought chiefly in automatic speech or writing, which seems in so many cases to express the personalities of deceased human beings. So faithfully are such personalities thus portrayed that many hundreds of cultured men and women have become convinced that these " automatic messages " are what they so often seem and claim to be, namely, messages formulated in the still surviving minds of deceased persons, and somehow expressed through the medium of the automatic writer. Those whose first impulse is to dismiss this conception with a sneer should try to abstain from this course, until they have first-hand acquaintance with instances of this strange phenomenon. On the other hand, a hasty acceptance of this interpretation of the facts is equally to be deprecated. For the evaluation of the evidence is a most delicate and difficult work, requiring complete freedom from bias ; yet the number of persons who are capable of maintaining the attitude of impartial inquiry in the face of this evidence seems to be but a minute fraction of the cultivated world.

Empirical support for the belief in communion with the divine mind is sought along two lines chiefly. First, it is argued that the process of religious conversion is often one which cannot be accounted for in terms of the known properties of the human mind in general and of the mental peculiarities of the persons concerned. Secondly, it is pointed out that in all ages the specifically religious experiences of men, even of men brought up under the influence of the most diverse traditions, have certain features in common which mark them as the work of a common influence and point to their determination from a common source. Hence, it is argued, it is reasonable to believe that this religious experience, of which the fullest or completest type is the mystical sense of the absorption of the self in a larger whole, is what it appears to be to those who best know it ; namely, an actual union or communion of the human mind with the divine mind. This reasoning has been urged in modern times by a number of writers, but by none so forcibly as by the late William James in his celebrated treatise, *The Varieties of Religious Experience.* The influence of that work has been very great; and to it is largely due the fact that psychology, which until very recently was commonly regarded with hostile suspicion by the leaders of religious thought, as well as by the rank and file, seems now in a fair way to become the chosen handmaid of theology and even its principal support. For, since the publication of that book, there has sprung up what may almost be called a new branch of literature in the shape of several journals and a stream of articles and books devoted to the psychology of religious experience and written for the most part by theologians.

It will be seen from this brief review of the field of abnormal psychology that in most of its branches we are compelled to recognize the reality of subconscious mental operations; and that though the results both in behaviour and in consciousness of such operations are often similar to those of normal mental process, yet in many cases these results go beyond the normal.

More than one attempt has been made to

devise an hypothesis which will bring all these supernormal effects under one explanation. Of such attempts the most interesting, perhaps, is that of William James. He suggested that we may regard all minds as connected in some immediate fashion which permits of their reciprocal influence and of the conjunction of their powers; or, to put the notion in another way, that all mind, human and infra-human as well as superhuman mind, is one, and that our individual minds are but partial manifestations of the one mind, conditioned by the peculiarities of our bodily organisms. All the supernormal effects of mental action, including the extremer instances of control of bodily processes, the expression of knowledge not acquired by any normal means, the supreme achievements of genius, religious conversion, and the ecstatic sense of absorption of the self in a larger all-comprehensive whole, which seems to be the extreme form of the specifically religious experience—all these effects might then be attributed to a partial or temporary suspension of the conditions which commonly isolate the individual mind.

No open-minded student of psychology will refuse to recognize the legitimacy and the fascination of such speculations. But the chief work of abnormal psychology must continue to be impartial observation and critical sifting of the empirical data, on the basis of which alone such speculations can be tested or verified.

CHAPTER VIII

SOCIAL PSYCHOLOGY

WHEN the student of behaviour has learnt from the various departments of Psychology, reviewed in the foregoing pages, all they can teach him of the structure, genesis, and modes of operation of the individual mind, a large field still awaits his exploration. If we put aside as unproven such speculations as that touched on at the end of the foregoing chapter, and refuse to admit any modes of communication or influence between minds other than through the normal channels of sense-perception and bodily movement, we must nevertheless recognize the existence in a certain sense of over-individual or collective minds.

We may fairly define a mind as an organized system of mental or purposive forces; and, in the sense so defined, every highly organized human society may properly be said to possess a collective mind. For the collective actions which constitute the history of any such society are conditioned by an organization which can only be described in terms of mind, and which yet is not comprised within the mind of any individual; the society is rather constituted by the system of relations obtaining between the individual minds which are its units of composition. Under any given circumstances the actions of the society are, or may be, very different from the mere sum of the actions with which its several members would react to the situation in the absence of the system of relations which renders them a society; or, in other words, the thinking and acting of each man, in so far as he thinks and acts as a member of a society, is very different from his thinking and acting as an isolated individual.

We shall presently consider more nearly what is implied in this proposition. But first it may be pointed out that, if we recognize the existence of collective minds, the work of social psychology falls under three heads. The one head is the study of the general principles of collective psychology, that is, the study of the general principles of collective thinking and feeling and acting, as displayed by men in social groups. Secondly, the general principles of collective psychology being given, there remains the study of the peculiarities presented by the collective behaviour and mental life of particular societies. Thirdly, the mental life of any society with its socialized and organically related members being given, social psychology has to describe the way in which each new member entering the society becomes moulded to its traditional ways of thinking, feeling, and doing, until he is fit to play his part as a member and to contribute his influence to its collective mental life.

This third division of the field of social psychology overlaps and supplements in an important manner the study of the development of the individual mind. For, though it is possible to study this development in abstraction from the social setting of the individual, and to establish in this way certain laws of mental development, any such study must be in many respects incomplete and misleading. Every normal human being grows up under the constant influence of the society into which he is born, and his mental development is moulded by it at every point. He becomes the heir to an intellectual and moral tradition which has slowly been built up, bit by bit, through the efforts of thousands of generations. Even in the most primitive societies of savage men this tradition is already very extensive and complex ; and in our modern civilized societies it has advanced so

H

far in these respects that no one mind can absorb more than a relatively small fraction of the whole. Of the intellectual tradition the most important part is language, the instrument and condition of almost all further acquirement. In acquiring the command of his native language a child has much more to learn than the adult who sets out to master a foreign tongue. For, while the latter has to do little more than to attach a new sound to some familiar object, the child, in learning to use words, is learning also to break up the whole world of his environment into a multitude of things, and to discern a multitude of distinctions and relations between them. All these things, distinctions and relations, are but a selection from the infinite number which might be discerned by an all-powerful mind. The child makes a selection which is in the main that which is the basis of the culture of his society ; and in making this selection he is largely influenced by the language created by his forefathers, in order to mark these selected aspects of the world. The normal child acquires also from his social group a great number of traditional beliefs about the objects which he has been led to recognize ; most of which he continues to hold throughout his life, without ever questioning their truth or inquiring how he came to accept them. And in civilized societies he may acquire also the command of all, or some of, the powerful instruments of the intellect which have been built up by the labours of many generations, such instruments as written language, drawing, numbers, and mathematical knowledge.

A more important part, perhaps, of the individual's social heritage is the moral tradition. Each one of us has to make this his own, not merely by acquiring knowledge of it, but by building up a system of moral sentiments; for it is questionable whether these are in any degree transmitted by heredity; and even if a certain basis of the moral sentiments is thus transmitted, it is certain that much of the moral tradition has to be impressed anew upon each child, in order that he may become capable of controlling his behaviour in accordance with the moral code of his community.

The preparation of the individual to play his proper part in the life of his community involves, then, a vast amount of shaping of his mental development by the influence of society; the understanding of this shaping process is clearly a matter of some importance. In so far as men have deliberately attempted to promote this process, they have acted upon theories which, especially as regards the shaping of the character, have generally been of the most inadequate kind. From the ancients who taught that knowledge and virtue are identical, to Rousseau, the English Utilitarians, and Herbert Spencer, the intellectualist and the hedonist fallacies, generally combined, have vitiated almost all theories of the process; and man has been persistently represented as doing right because he realizes that honesty is the best policy. The practical outcome of all such theories is an undue reliance upon rewards and punishments and the prospect of pleasure or of pain, as regulators of conduct.

Only a sounder psychology can save us from these fallacies. We must sweep away every trace of the doctrine that conduct proceeds essentially from a calculation of satisfactions to be yielded by this or that course; and we must put in its place the truth that every creature, whether animal, child, or man, behaves in this or that way, because the impulses with which he is innately endowed are set towards this or that end. From this it follows that the problem of moral education is the problem of directing the impulses towards appropriate objects, or, in technical terms, of linking the appropriate conative and cognitive dispositions. This cannot be achieved by any system of rewards and punishments, but only by a much more subtly working influence of society upon the developing individual. We must recognize that, in the influencing of the development of both the cognitive and the conative sides of the mind, logical reasoning plays but a secondary and occasional rôle, and that the processes by which society works upon the growing mind at every moment of its waking life are of a very different nature.

These processes may be classed under three great heads—suggestion, sympathy, and imitation. By " suggestion " we mean the process in virtue of which beliefs are induced in, or communicated to, the subject independently of all logical reasoning to a conclusion. We tend to accept without question the beliefs we find established in the minds of our fellows ; and to this tendency each of us owes by far the greater part of the beliefs which constitute the working capital of his intellect ; even when we reason with strictest logic, we commonly reason from premises which are beliefs acquired in this unreasoning fashion.

By " sympathy " we mean the tendency to experience, in face of the same object, the same emotions and impulses that are revealed by the behaviour of our fellows. By the working of this principle the set of our impulses is regulated and brought into conformity with the moral tradition, or, in other words, the growth of our moral sentiments is directed.

By " imitation " we mean the tendency to direct in detail the bodily movements to which our impulses prompt us, according to the pattern set us by our fellows ; a tendency not without importance, though less profoundly influential than the other two.

The elucidation of the subtle workings of these principles is the chief task of the one branch of social psychology. Here it must suffice to have indicated merely the nature of that task, and to say that some progress has already been made with it.

In studying the general principles of collective psychology, we have to begin with the simplest forms of human and animal association ; for, although it is only the more highly developed human groups that can properly be said to manifest a collective mind, yet the modes of reciprocal influence of the individual and of the group, which are essential to the existence of the collective mind, are displayed in relatively simple forms by groups of low degrees of organization.

We must pass over the fascinating study of animal societies, noting merely the most important of its lessons ; namely, first, that the prime condition of the existence of animal societies is the gregarious instinct ; and

secondly, that the harmonious co-operation
of the members of the group, especially
in flight and in defence, is secured by the
tendency to sympathetic reaction which is innate in each member (see p. 166). This primitive sympathetic tendency, the reader may be
reminded, is merely an instinctive tendency
to respond to the expressions characteristic
of each of the principal innate impulses of
the species, with a similar impulse and emotional excitement. We see this principle
illustrated in the most perfect and simple
manner among the most social of all the
animals, namely, the hive bees. The removal
of the queen from the midst of her immediate
attendants produces in them a distress which
expresses itself in a peculiar note ; and this
note rapidly evokes a similar distress, similarly
expressed, throughout all the bees present
in the hive. The restoration of the queen (or
even of her dead body or of some object
impregnated with the odour of her body)
transforms the distress of the bees in her
immediate neighbourhood to a pleasurable
excitement, which in turn expresses itself
in a characteristic note and is rapidly spread
by the agency of this sound throughout the
hive. The note expressive of anger spreads
in like manner this excitement throughout
the hive ; and in all probability the same is

true of notes expressing other emotional impulses.

When we turn to consider the simplest form of human association, namely, the fortuitously collected crowd of men, we see that it owes its most striking peculiarities to this same sympathetic principle. The notorious characteristic of the crowd is the violence of the outbursts of the primary emotions and impulses. The panic is the simplest and most striking type of such collective excitement; it is displayed by human crowds just as simply and terribly as by animal groups. If some hundreds of men are gathered together in one place, and if some few of them are terrified and give audible and visible expression to their fear, the excitement is apt to spread almost instantaneously throughout the whole group; even though the object that primarily provoked it in the few remains hidden from the mass. And the excitement intensifies itself from moment to moment; because each man not only responds to the first cry of fear with a thrill of the same emotion, but also, as he looks round to discover the threatening danger, he sees fear expressed on every face and in every gesture, and hears it in every voice. Thus the emotion is propagated and accentuated by the primitive sympathetic tendency ; and with it the impulse to escape grows stronger, until it becomes uncontrollable and, dominating all members of the crowd, drives them on to those wild struggles to escape in which men seem to lose all the human attributes, and to sink back to the level of purely animal behaviour.

If the panic affords the most striking and terrible illustration of collective emotion, all the other crude emotions and impulses seem capable of being spread and intensified by the same process of sympathetic contagion. Anger especially is notoriously apt to spread through a crowd, and the angry mob is only less violent and less inaccessible to the voice of reason than the panic-stricken crowd. The achievements of great orators show how the whole range of the emotions may, under favourable conditions, be collectively evoked and intensified.

The intensity of the collective emotion of an unorganized crowd is favoured by the fact that each member of a crowd tends to lose to some extent his sense of personal identity and responsibility ; he no longer stands alone, an individual before the eyes of his fellow-men, but feels himself an undistinguishable unit of a mass on which, rather than on its units, the judgment of the rest of the world must be passed. Hence each man is apt to let himself go, to make little effort to control himself.

The emotional excitability of the crowd is very unfavourable to its intellectual processes ; for intense emotion renders men uncritical, hasty, biased in judgment, and easily led to belief by mere suggestion. The diminished sense of personal responsibility of the members of a crowd makes in the same direction. But the influence most deleterious to the quality of collective judgment and reasoning is what may be called *mass-suggestion*. Every man is to some extent suggestible ; every one is a little inclined to believe a proposition which is confidently made to him ; and, if the same proposition is made to him by a hundred or a thousand men, it becomes difficult for him to retain a critical attitude towards it. But now, when a great crowd acclaims a statement made by an orator, the proposition not only comes to each member as the accepted opinion of each of his fellow-members ; but the fact that these constitute a crowd, a vast whole impressive by reason of its mass, its power, its unknown possibilities, renders each man more suggestible, more ready to accept its opinions uncritically, than if he merely heard the same opinion expressed by the same number of individuals. The most striking illustration of this suggestibility of crowds is afforded by

many recorded instances of collective hallucination thus induced, instances in which all
or most of the members of a crowd have been
led to perceive objects that had no existence,
objects such as the sea-serpent, or a fiery cross,
or even a host of men or angels in the clouds.

By reason, then, of its emotional excitability, its high degree of suggestibility, and
the diminished sense of responsibility of its
members, the behaviour of the fortuitous
unorganized crowd is apt to be of a kind much
inferior to the average behaviour of its units
when they think and act as individuals.

Few crowds, however, are altogether fortuitous. A crowd is commonly brought together
by some common interest or purpose in the
minds of the individuals that compose it, a
common interest in sport, or music, or politics,
or religion, a common loyalty or a common
resentment. Any such crowd, then, is composed of less diverse units than a fortuitous
crowd : it may be said to possess a certain
homogeneity of composition in so far as its
units are possessed of common knowledge,
common opinions, and common sentiments.
Some degree of homogeneity is a necessary
condition of all collective mental process.
A fortuitous gathering of persons of various
nationalities, of various levels of culture,
speaking different languages and possessing

widely different opinions and sentiments, could display only the crudest of all forms of collective process, namely, the panic. And the more homogeneous is the crowd, the more capable is it of truly collective thinking and acting. But, so long as the crowd possesses no organization, its homogeneity will tend only to intensify the peculiarities of collective mental process that we have already noted.

Are we to conclude, then, that to share in collective mental life, to be a member of a group, is necessarily to suffer degradation of one's mental life? Such a conclusion (and it is often asserted or implied) would be a very serious error.

It is only by sharing in the collective life of organized societies that the mass of men is raised above a very low level of almost purely selfish behaviour; and it is through such sharing that great numbers of men are raised to a level of consistently public-spirited conduct and even to heights of heroic self-sacrifice.

The principal task of collective psychology is, then, to show how organization of societies produces this paradoxical result; namely, that, whereas the collective behaviour of the unorganized group implies a much lower level of mental process than the individual behaviour of its average units, and thus involves a degradation of its component individuals, the collective life of a well-organized society commonly attains a higher level, both intellectually and morally, than could be individually attained by its average members, and raises many of those who participate in it to much higher levels of thought and action.

A single example may serve to illustrate the fact and to indicate the lines along which the solution of the paradox is to be found. A well-organized patriot army, such as the Japanese armies that fought in the Russo-Japanese war, illustrates the facts most strikingly. The organization of such an army is relatively simple, yet in other respects it is of the highest type; for it is the product of deliberate design and of the voluntary acceptance and working out of the design by all its members. The movements of the whole army express a degree of intelligence which far surpasses that of its average members; namely, the intelligence of the commander-in-chief and of a highly selected and trained staff, deliberating and deciding with the aid of a vast amount of detailed information supplied by subordinates, and in the light of the knowledge of the principles of war accumulated by successive generations of mankind. The essential condition that raises the intellectual level of the collective behaviour of such an army is so obvious, that it may seem needless to state it in words ; it is such an organization as gives, to those best qualified to judge of any question, the decisive voice in the formation of opinion upon it. But it is no less true, though less obvious, that all collective deliberation and decision, whether of a committee, a parliament, or a whole nation, can only be saved from the imbecilities of the unorganized crowd by the existence of such an organization as gives predominant influence and responsibility to those members best qualified for arriving at just conclusions. It may be added that the extreme simplicity and effectiveness of the organization of the army on its intellectual side is only rendered possible by the fact, that the collective action of the group is directed towards a single end, which end is perfectly defined and is accepted and willed by every member of the group ; namely, the ultimate defeat of the enemy.

On the moral side also the collective life of such an army rises to a high level in virtue of its organization. It is true that it owes much to the fact that a common purpose animates all its members ; for even an unorganized mob animated by a common purpose, such as a lynching mob, may display a considerable degree of resolution. The moral force displayed by an army depends also in large measure upon sympathetic intensification of emotion ; though, as the liability of almost all armies to panic shows, sympathetic contagion may work adversely also.

But the main condition of the attainment by the army of a high moral level is the existence of the group-spirit. By the group-spirit we mean the existence in each soldier's mind of a clear knowledge or idea of the army and of his place in it and of his part in its life, accompanied by a sentiment of devotion to it. It is the existence in each mind of this sentiment that alone renders possible a truly collective volition ; it is this which sustains each man throughout long months of fatigue and discomfort and which plays a part of decisive importance at each critical moment of battle, as when the charging line wavers under the hail of bullets. And in the wisely organized army, the group-spirit is not single but multiple ; each man entertains not only a sentiment of devotion to the army as a whole, which leads him to desire its success and glory, but also similar sentiments for his corps, his regiment, his company, which lead him to desire, and to do his utmost to achieve, the success and glory of each of these groups with which he identifies himself, in friendly rivalry with the similar groups. For it is a most beneficent characteristic of the group-sentiment, that devotion to any group is perfectly compatible with, and even favourable to the strength of, a similar sentiment for any larger group that comprises the lesser. The development of the group-spirit, the influence upon it of traditions, and symbols, and territorial grouping, and so forth, are therefore of great importance for the military psychologist, with whom it lies to display the principal conditions of success and of failure in war.

Yet another condition of high morality is secured for an army, if it is so organized that the men with the firmest courage and finest enthusiasm occupy the positions of greatest prestige ; for then their temper will inspire those who stand next to them, and will be transmitted by these downwards through the whole system.

These are a few of the psychological principles by the operation of which the collective life of the group may be raised far above that of the unorganized crowd. It must be noticed that the basal principles of all collective life, namely, sympathetic contagion, mass-suggestion, and imitation, are not suspended in the well-organized group ; they work in it as strongly as in the crowd, but their operation is modified and turned wholly to good.

The study of other types of organized groups, the savage tribe, the secret society, the political party, or the trade-union, enables us to elaborate these fundamental principles and to supplement them with others of less importance ; and in this way collective psychology prepares itself to gain some understanding of the most complex, interesting, and important form of collective mind ; namely, the mind of a modern nation-state.

The phrase " national character " is in common use ; but those who use it seldom make clear in which of its two senses they mean it to be understood. Perhaps it is commonly meant to denote the character of some hypothetical individual who may be regarded as the type or average representative of the nation. But the other meaning of the phrase must be clearly distinguished from this. A nation with a long past and a vast system of living traditions and institutions has a character which is not by any means merely the sum or resultant of the characters of all its component units. For this character is largely determined by these traditions and institutions ; and these are the joint product of the characters of the individuals of foregoing generations and of the historical circumstances of the life of the nation through many centuries. In the same sense and for the same reasons, a nation has also a collective national intellect as well as a collective national character.

The application of the principles of collective psychology to the understanding of the lives of particular nations, or of other historical groups, constitutes the third field of social psychology. In this great field of research psychology cannot walk alone, but has to co-operate with other sciences, especially political history and economic science ; and the proper division of the work between these several studies and the science of sociology is at present a hotly disputed problem. Without entering into that difficult question, we may insist that, in the interpretation of the life of nations, the application of the principles of collective mental life is not the whole of the psychological work that has to be done.

There remains for the psychologist the work of describing the mental peculiarities of the individuals that compose the various nations and the classes within them, and especially he has to try to define the innate peculiarities of their mental constitutions. That is to say, collective psychology has to invoke the aid of the comparative psychology of races and classes, before it can hope to accomplish its proper share in the interpretation of history and in accounting for the peculiarities of the collective life of each nation. For, however great the influence of traditions, of institutions, and of economic conditions, in determining the course of life and the success or failure of a nation, the innate qualities of the population will make themselves felt and, in the long run, will exert a preponderant influence over all other factors.

Here we have an immense field awaiting exploration. Much has been written on the innate mental peculiarities of races and nations; but hitherto we have little more than vague, though generally dogmatic, expressions of opinion, unsupported by any attempt at exact observation, and, for the most part, expressed by writers who have not even grasped the nature of the problems to be solved. The tasks immediately confronting the psychologist in this field are, then, the definition of the problems and the working out of methods by which they may be profitably attacked.

The prime difficulty of all work in this field is that of distinguishing between the innate and the acquired mental structure, to which reference was made in an earlier chapter. But the comparative study of peoples may throw light on this question, and is perhaps more capable of doing so than any other method of approaching it. For, since the innate

qualities of any people, constantly and generation after generation, exert a shaping and
selective influence upon the growth of its
culture and institutions, we may expect to
find them reflected there. This, then, is one
of the tasks of comparative racial psychology.
But its main work must be the description of
the innate mental peculiarities of races and
peoples. We want to know just what are the
differences in regard to mental endowment
between the Yellow, the Black, and the White
races, between the Celt and the Teuton and
the Slav, the Arab and the Jew and the
Armenian. We want to know how these
differences have been produced. We want to
know the effect upon innate mental structure
of the crossing of races, and whether populations formed by the crossing of races can
properly be said to form in course of time
new stable sub-races. We want also to know
whether any differences of innate mental
quality obtain between the various sections
and social strata of our great complex national
societies. And especially we want to know
what changes, if any, are being brought about
in the innate mental constitution of these
populations under their present conditions;
whether, as some assert, various forms of
social selection are making strongly for
deterioration; or whether, as is commonly

believed, the civilized stocks continue to evolve a higher type of mental structure ; or lastly, whether the principal change being effected is not a greater differentiation, resulting in the production of a comparatively low-grade mass of population at one end of the scale, and of a number of stocks of exceptional ability and moral stamina at the other. All these are questions that must be answered in detail, before we can build up a true science of society, a science that will point the way to such a political and social organization as will offer some guarantee of stability and some prospect of the continued progress of human mind and human culture.

All these problems fall within the province of psychology, and can be solved only through the progress of that science.

believed, the civilized stocks continue to evolve a higher type of mental structure; or lastly, whether the principal change being effected is not a greater differentiation, resulting in the production of a comparatively low-grade mass of population at one end of the scale, and of a number of stocks of exceptional ability and moral stamina at the other. All these are questions that must be answered in detail, before we can build up a true science of society, a science that will point the way to such a political and social organization as will offer some guarantee of stability and some prospect of the continued progress of human mind and human culture.

All these problems fall within the province of psychology, and can be solved only through the progress of that science.

BIBLIOGRAPHY

BIBLIOGRAPHY

FOR GENERAL SURVEY

WILLIAM JAMES : *Principles of Psychology* (Macmillan & Co.).

G. F. STOUT : *Manual of Psychology* (Clive & Co.).

JAMES WARD : *Art. " Psychology," Ency. Brit.*

WM. McDOUGALL : *Body and Mind* (Methuen & Co.).

EXPERIMENTAL AND PHYSIOLOGICAL PSYCHOLOGY

C. S. MYERS : *Introduction to Experimental Psychology* (Camb. Univ. Press).

G. T. LADD and R. S. WOODWORTH : *Elements of Physiological Psychology* (Scribner).

WM. McDOUGALL : *Primer of Physiological Psychology* (Dent).

G. M. STRATTON : *Experimental Psychology and its Bearing on Culture* (Macmillan & Co.).

MENTAL DEVELOPMENT AND EVOLUTION

L. T. HOBHOUSE : *Mind in Evolution*
(Macmillan & Co.).

W. M. KEATINGE : *Suggestion in Education*
(A. & C. Black).

STANLEY HALL : *Adolescence* (Appleton & Co.).

James Sully : *Teacher's Handbook of Psychology*
(Longmans).
R. R. Marett : *Anthropology* (Home University
Library).

THE ANIMAL MIND

C. Lloyd Morgan : *Animal Behaviour* (Arnold).
G. W. & E. G. Peckham : *Wasps, Social and Solitary*
(Constable & Co.).
E. L. Thorndike : *Animal Intelligence* (Macmillan).
M. F. Washburn : *The Animal Mind* (Macmillan).

THE ABNORMAL

F. W. H. Myers : *Human Personality and its Sur-
vival of Bodily Death* (abridged ed., Longmans).
A. Moll : *Hypnotism* (Contemporary Science Series).
William James : *The Varieties of Religious Experi-
ence* (Longmans).
Bernard Hart : *Abnormal Psychology*
(Camb. Univ. Press).
Morton Prince and other writers : *Psychother-
apeutics* (Fisher Unwin).
Sir W. F. Barrett : *Psychical Research*
(Home University Library).

SOCIAL PSYCHOLOGY

Graham Wallas : *Human Nature in Politics*
(Constable & Co.).
Wm. McDougall : *An Introduction to Social
Psychology* (Methuen & Co.).
G. le Bon : *The Crowd* (Fisher Unwin).
E. A. Ross : *Social Psychology* (Macmillan).

INDEX

249

Printed in Great Britain by Butler & Tanner Ltd., Frome and London

THE
HOME UNIVERSITY LIBRARY
OF MODERN KNOWLEDGE

* *Revised* 1928–9.

History

Literature

* *Revised* 1928–9.

Political and Social Science

Religion and Philosophy

Revised 1928-9.

Complete List up to Spring, 1929.   New titles will be added yearly.